POTENTIAL

Leveraging Your Past for the Professional and Personal Success You Deserve

BY BARBARA POLK

Potential: Leveraging Your Past for the Professional and Personal Success You Deserve

By Barbara Polk

Printed and manufactured in the United States of America.

978-1-955750-01-1 PRINT

978-1-955750-02-8 - EBOOK

www.networlding.com

Contents

Introduction

"We write for the same reason that we walk, talk, climb mountains or swim the oceans—because we can. We have some impulse within us that makes us want to explain ourselves to other human beings." ~ **Maya Angelou**

Did I dream too big, or not big enough? Did I learn from my mistakes and successes, or did I move on to the next one without thinking, hoping luck or chance would save me from the next challenge? When I look back at my life, is it with regret, depression, nostalgia, pride, or satisfaction?

Most of us ask these very personal, private questions at some time, either early on, in middle age, or, for many of us, not until we're on our deathbed. I chose to ask these questions now. And I chose to answer them in a very public book based on a giant leap of faith that you'll find wisdom or, at the very least, entertainment in my mistakes, successes, and, most importantly, lessons learned.

I hope through this book that I can reinforce for you that life has been, is, and always will be a journey we were meant to take. Whether your childhood was a struggle or adulthood has held its challenges, you can actually become resilient by healing from trauma and learning from mistakes. Struggles can fuel a desire to strive for different outcomes or teach you what not to do.

> *"Do not let the memories of your past limit the potential of your future. There are no limits to what you can achieve on your journey through life, except in your mind."* ~ **Roy T. Bennett**, *The Light in the Heart*

It's rare that self-awareness just happens. It takes reflection—and perhaps a degree of maturity and a desire to evolve. Regardless of what age you are, there is life lived behind you. Whether you're twentysomething or sixty something, patterns and behaviors are difficult to decode.

As an executive coach and corporate executive, I've found through working with a wide variety of clients and colleagues that we all have pasts we need to fully explore and learn from if we're to continue to mature and succeed.

Your life may mirror many of the events I describe, or not. Whether your pathways are similar to mine or not, I trust that you'll explore your life and experiences to discover your own wisdom and wounds, no matter how painful they are or were. They're yours, precious for what they've contributed to who you are today.

Everything that happens to you is a gift, a resource you can use in the future. Some of those gifts may come wrapped in poverty, shame, or unrealized potential, while others may come in glittering, dazzling packages that promise much but deliver little. You never know at the time the role any experience—good or bad—will have in your life.

That's why it's important to pay attention and find the lessons, insights, and gifts as soon as you can. It's easier when you frame a negative event as quickly as possible as a lesson rather than as a trauma or mistake. Reflecting and understanding what lessons I can derive from the past has taken me years to master, but that's fine. I've learned it's an ongoing process, a work in progress—as it is for us all.

Throughout this book I'll share a wide variety of my stories to help illustrate my most useful lessons. I've also inserted research that adds validation and further insights to the lessons.

I hope my stories, experiences, and insights speak to you in some way. I hope the lessons I learned will show you that no matter what your challenges or life events are, you can overcome them. Whether you invest in therapy, coaching, or even education, you can leverage every aspect of your life, good or bad, to have the future you deserve.

PART 1

Childhood 101

CHAPTER 1

Starting at the Beginning

Our childhood certainly shapes the adult we become, but we can't let past traumas or circumstances overshadow the future we deserve to have.

Chapter Soundtrack: "Chapel of Love" ~
The Dixie Cups, 1964

My mom, Lorraine, was eighteen, and my dad, Robert, was twenty-one when they got married. However, it wasn't exactly young love that drove them to the wedding altar. I was the reason their parents insisted they get married. In their Black, churchgoing, working-class families, having a baby outside marriage was a huge embarrassment to the entire family—not just to the single mother.

My maternal grandfather proudly boasted that he called my paternal grandfather and said, "There aren't going to be any bastards in my family." And there weren't.

However, there was trauma, domestic violence, alcohol and drug abuse, and dysfunction. But there was love too.

A wedding at city hall was quickly arranged after Lor-raine's condition was discovered. Immediately after the ceremony, my dad returned to his service in Vietnam. My mom lived at home with her parents and her newborn baby—me, named Barbara after my father's mother.

The traditional concept of marriage that my parents were ushered into, while not ill intended, resulted in a marriage that was not based on healthy choices. Societal, religious, and even cultural pressures dictated choices or norms that weren't truly beneficial for either of them.

A healthier choice would have been one where both par-ties knew their partner extraordinarily well and were mature enough to make a joint decision. However, neither my mother's nor my father's preferences were valued. My mother particularly, as a pregnant teen, felt very little if any personal power. I find it sad that even today marriage is romanticized as the best option for a woman or as a magical, romantic adventure rather than a complicated relationship that can be ripe for conflict and requires high levels of trust and enormous compromise.

> ***But change has occurred since the 1960s***
>
> *Research shows that adults are marrying later in life, while the numbers of adults cohabiting and rais-ing children outside of marriage have dramatically increased. The age of couples entering a first marriage*

> *tends to average 27 for women and 29 for men. This is a sharp uptick from 1960's stats of age 20 for women and 23 for men. About a quarter (24%) of never-married young adults between the ages 25 to 34 today are living with a partner.* [1]

Marriage didn't solve my parents' problem beyond giving me and my extended family the respect due a duly wedded couple and their child. It didn't contribute to creating a healthy family. As a result of my father's addictions and my mother's introverted nature, my childhood was very tumultuous.

When I look back, I can see that my family's dysfunction formed the foundation of both the lifelong anxiety I've contended with and, ironically, the resilience of my adulthood. The steady resilience I've tapped into time and time again wouldn't have existed without my childhood. That's what this book is about—the gifts that are given to us through our conflicts. But we usually don't recognize them until we're further down the road. If you haven't recognized the most significant gifts your past gave you, I hope this helps you recognize how wealthy you probably are. It took me a while to see that, but it's there.

I realize now how fortunate I was that I also experienced a great deal of affection and attention from my extended family. I took that for granted as a child and young adult. It wasn't until much later that I realized how their love formed the foundation and anchor from which I would create my own life.

I say my parents marrying was a bad choice—and there were *many* bad times—but not everything about my parents' courtship and marriage was horrible. In the beginning their story is quite moving. My mother met my father when her brother brought him home from army boot camp. The Vietnam War was the background to a rapid courtship.

My dad was tall, charismatic, and handsome, with an irreverent sense of humor and an infectious laugh. This is probably why, as his life unfolded, he could get away with abusive behavior that included low accountability, alcohol use, drug use—you name it. But he was very likeable, and my mother fell in love with him—including all his faults, many of which I'm sure she didn't discover or experience until I came along.

My mother was a very kindhearted person who tended to be passive. She hated conflict. As such, she rarely raised her voice. She felt conflict could be *messy*—and she was right. It often was. I believe if she would have built the courage to speak up, she would have been able to get more of what she wanted and certainly deserved in life. She was also very intelligent, a voracious reader, and a good writer.

If she had been encouraged to continue her education or been in the position to do so, she could have pursued a variety of careers. The bottom line here is that I'm a mixture of both my parents, which goes to show that you can't outrun your genetic makeup.

Speaking of genetic makeup, in the South, and especially among Black families, love is expressed through food. For Black families, family dinner or supper is a time when memories are created; support, love, and family gossip are shared; traditions are reinforced; and new bonds are made. I know I was loved because when I was six months old, my pediatrician put me on a diet because I was overweight.

My grandmother fed me solid food as an infant. Just like the good Southern woman she was, she made sure I ate everything the family was eating for dinner. The only difference was that my servings were chopped up in small bits.

What I was served up daily could have been collard greens, chicken, ham, or cornbread with a little bit of potlikker. Potlikker is the liquid left behind after you boil collard greens, mustard greens, or turnip greens. To my pediatrician, this wasn't healthy eating. To my grandmother and my aunts, it was love. In my baby pictures I bear an uncanny resemblance to a sumo wrestler.

By all accounts, I was very bonded to my mother. She carried me on her hip everywhere, and I slept in bed with her until I was one year old. If she left me for any reason, even with my beloved Grandmother Anna Mae, I would cry incessantly until she returned. My mother's sisters—Josephine, Renee, and Nina—were also very pivotal in my life.

And while up until this point it sounds like I had a pretty idyllic life—surrounded by strong, loving women—it wouldn't take long for the proverbial wrench to be thrown into the works. My father returned from Vietnam after being honorably discharged and got a job as a police officer. My brother, Robbie, was born when I was three years old. We were well on our way to embodying the American dream. Or so it seemed from the outside.

Dad worked crazy hours and night shifts, and he wasn't successful in meeting his obligations to his family. Unfortunately, like many Vietnam veterans, he'd also come home traumatized and suffering from PTSD. His PTSD and inability to cope with the stresses of the racism, war, marriage, children, and work led him to become a recreational drug user.

> Studies show that regardless of whatever war or conflict they were in, many veterans have marital problems, and, as a result, family violence is common. They are also often emotionally detached from themselves and others, and they can be erratic and unpredictable in their interactions with family. "

Unfortunately, my father's behaviors followed the classic pattern of domestic violence:

1. The building of tension
2. An incident of abuse
3. Reconciliation
4. Calm

The pattern then repeats over time, with each cycle often more severe than the last.

> *While many of the descriptions of domestic violence that make the news tend to revolve around physical violence, abuse can also include financial control, threats of sexual violence, humiliation, and verbal degradation. These tendencies or behaviors move into the workplace, where they can play out with employees or managers. In the workplace, codependency often appears in the form of a dominant boss or coworker who exerts control over a more submissive employee. This is a dysfunctional workplace dynamic. Does this description inspire any a-ha moments?*

My father also fell into a pattern of infidelity. It didn't take long for divorce to follow. My mom was twenty-six when she found herself a single parent with two children to raise. Certainly, lots of children grow up with divorced parents and dysfunction, but these dynamic shapes all of us differently. To me, my mom was a dreamer. All she ever wanted was a traditional family, a home, and a husband. Unfortunately, she didn't have the fairy-tale life she fantasized about.

CHAPTER 2

Mom

"You may not control all the events that happen to you. But you can decide not to be reduced by them." ~ **Maya Angelou**

Chapter Soundtrack: "A Song for Mama" ~ Boyz II Men, 1996

Marriage to my father was a rollercoaster of emotions for my mother. I have memories of my parents dancing together and laughing, as well as memories of my father towering over my mother and yelling at the top of his lungs. My mother hated conflict, and her response was to cry and retreat, then lastly to turn inward—speaking to no one. She later described herself as being depressed, withdrawn, and struggling to care for her children during that time.

Eventually, my mother understood what her family had already concluded: she needed to leave my father.

Women stay in abusive, unhealthy relationships because of damaged perspectives of self-worth, financial insecurity, and, of course, the desire to cling to a false fairy-tale image of the relationship they want to have. Their thoughts become distorted. Women in these types of relationships need patient counsel and the support of their families, which, fortunately, my mother had.

Leaving was not an easy choice, as she had never had a job and didn't even know how to drive a car. My mother would be dependent upon her parents for everything while she rebuilt her life. She was struggling with depression, so that first year she separated from my father was rough.

Initially, I lived with my mother's oldest sister as I started kindergarten, while my brother stayed with my mother and grandparents. Although I saw my mother frequently, I rarely saw my father. I remember feeling abandoned and bewildered by all of the changes. Fortunately, my mother stabilized with counseling and support, and we began to live together again.

I've learned that when a child is separated from their parent or primary caregiver—and in my case, a sibling as well—this instability can cause anxiety, depression, and stress. However, if mental health resources are available, it's possible to learn to redirect the pain or harness the resilience built from those experiences and have a healthy life.

Most people know the statistics: almost 50% of all marriages in the United States will end in divorce or separation. For Black families, 65% of children live

> *with a single parent. The economic impact is shocking and can often result in a slide into poverty. The resulting instability and childhood trauma also can cause anxiety or depression even into adulthood because the early coping mechanism of the body and mind persists.*[iii]

From my adult perspective, I've often wondered how in the world my mother got through all of the challenges of her young adult life. I had my first daughter when I was thirty-one, and I had my twins when I was thirty-three. I felt overwhelmed and could often be in an inpatient mindset with them. So many times, I have thought, *Holy crap! How did my mother do this with far less maturity and experience, and not the same resources I had?* It has really made me feel for her.

My dad never paid my mother any child support, so we struggled financially during my childhood. Ultimately, my mother enrolled in secretarial school and worked for over thirty years at a well-known insurance company. She started as an entry-level clerk and rose through the ranks to a senior claims representative role. Even so, shopping with coupons and relying on food stamps with hope as a strategy permeates my childhood memories.

However, living in a semirural area allowed us to benefit from my grandmother's large garden. Fresh beans, tomatoes, and even grapes from a carefully tended arbor supplemented our food supply. My grandmother put up homemade preserves and jellies, and canned vegetables, while my grandfather and uncles fished and filled family members' freezers with their catch. We were never hungry thanks to our communal family structure.

> *My grandparents were survivors—particularly my grandmother. Having grown up in the South, she knew that gardening and pooling family resources was smart. It allowed them to support the family (and extended family) with minimal income.*
>
> Food insecurity is a critical problem, particularly for single parents. Think about supporting community gardens[IV] [V]:

Single motherhood was tough on my mom, and her somewhat introverted personality made it even more complicated. If she knew you, she could be quite talkative but was often quiet in large groups. There was an innocence about her as well, for example, she was a very voluptuous woman. She would wear bikinis at the beach or a pool, and my brother and I would stand guard as her protectors against any male attention. She was oblivious to all of it, but Robbie and I could tell if someone was paying her more attention than usual.

My mother was mostly observational, often with her head in a book. She was reluctant to advocate on her behalf in most situations. Perhaps because of this, I always felt emotionally stronger than my mother. I felt a need to protect her—to take care of her and my brother. My mother's vulnerability felt as tangible to me as a coat she wore. In many ways, she was a child herself, trying to raise two kids. Because she needed my support, I had to grow up fast rather than express the typical neediness of a young child.

> *"It is not uncommon for the oldest sibling in the case of divorce to take on a caregiver role. There can be some benefits to this, sometimes siblings are closer because of it. However, sometimes the oldest child takes on more adult responsibility than a child should."*[VI]

Fortunately, I was a strong-willed and determined child by all accounts. I loved school and devoured books. The library was my favorite place as a young girl. I remember crying if I didn't get an A on a quiz or test. I was that annoying kid who had a hand up for every question. To me, getting good grades became a way of identifying myself in a positive way—another type of strength that I owned and could control.

My clothes may have been from K-Mart and my sneakers a generic brand, but I was winning at school. My goal was to make sure everyone was happy with me at schoolteachers, administrators, cafeteria ladies ... You get the picture. At an early age, I also had an awareness of being "other."

Due to some fluke in school zoning, my brother and I went to a predominantly White school district. It was 1977, and there were very few Black children in any of my classrooms. I was often the only person of color. I was acutely aware that my Afro puffs and braids were different and that I had a special card for free lunch.

I remember *Roots*, the miniseries, was on TV that year. White children were calling me and the few other Black children "slaves" on the playground or trying to boss us around as if they were better than us. This infuriated me. I watched *Roots* intently every night—horrified but unable to look away from what I was seeing. It explained a lot to me about why there was a sense that being Black was somehow "less than" even if I received better grades. In protest, I decided that I would no longer stand up and recite the Pledge of Allegiance (Colin Kaepernick parallel notwithstanding).

Each morning in homeroom we were required to stand up and recite, and I refused. My teacher didn't know what to make of my defiance. She tried to cajole me into following the rules, but I wouldn't comply. Frustrated, she sent me to the principal's office. The principal was actually a very insightful person and seemed to understand I was expressing outrage, not actually trying to be a bad student. He talked to me patiently and ask me to reconsider my position, but I wouldn't.

Finally, after three trips to the principal's office, they contacted my mother, who had to leave work to come and get me, as I was being sent home. The next day I was allowed to return to school, and I did the same thing. This time my mother was nearly in tears when she arrived. She said, "Barbara, I can't keep leaving my job like this. I'll get in trouble!" I agreed to end my protest, but I then refused to sit in the rear of the classroom. Our seating was alphabetical, and Ps sat in the rear. Now I was having my Rosa Parks moment. At this point the teacher just left me alone.

> *"I have learned over the years that when one's mind is made up this diminishes fear; knowing what must be done does away with fear."* ~ **Rosa Parks**

I hated being different. Children can be cruel and are the products of what their parents say and do. So I didn't get invited to parties or to play after school because classmates weren't allowed to have me over. Frankly, there weren't enough other Black children close to us, so my brother and cousins were my playmates. If you don't meet the standards of beauty, success, or popularity—or even if your teachers look different than you and your differences are reinforced—it can impact your self-esteem. I was the perfect example of this.

> *In a 1954 study, Doctors Mamie and Kenneth Clark conducted "The Doll Test." The Clarks handed Black children four dolls. The dolls were identical except that two had dark-colored skin and two had light-colored skin. The Clarks asked the children questions, such as, Which dolls are nice? Which dolls are bad? Which doll is most like you?*
>
> *The results of the test showed that the majority of Black children preferred the White dolls over the Black*

> *dolls, saying the Black dolls were "bad" and that the White dolls looked most like them.*[VII]

I experienced some bullying in elementary school and middle school. I put up with a lot of racial slurs and comments on my hair and clothes, but if cornered, I would explode. I knew I was going to get in trouble, so it was only when the hurt had built up to a certain level that I couldn't help but act—particularly if someone bullied my little brother.

Once the other kids knew I would fight back, the bullying mostly subsided. Over time I learned to manage the frustration and cope with the pain. This was partially out of necessity because the consequence of fighting could be great for my brother and me.

My family members, whose childhood experiences sadly mirrored my own, were supportive and gave me constant moral support that helped me survive the daily stress. I processed that being bullied was less of a reflection on me and more a reflection on troubled and ignorant children who would soon be in my rearview mirror.

I did, however, have some allies among my classmates because of my grandparents' prolific garden. My grandparents would give gifts of tomatoes, zucchini, or corn to their neighbors. So those kids would often tell other kids to leave my brother and me alone, and they would sometimes ask us to join in on games at recess.

I recall that I hated gym class when we learned square dancing. None of the little White boys wanted me as a partner. I would outwardly act as if I didn't care, but it hurt me. *Am I not pretty enough? Am I less worthy? Are only little White girls pretty?* I wondered.

As a result, at school I learned to fit in and tried to dress and speak like the majority of my peers, hoping to gain some form of acceptance. I rejected my Blackness at school and waited until I got home to be the true Barbara. I thought this strategy was the way to avoid the constant stress of my otherness. I learned early how to code-switch, to try to blend in as much as possible.

> *I discovered that academic accomplishments and good behavior win praise and privileges. People made assumptions about my abilities, and I wanted to prove them wrong. For many people of color, code-switching is a survival technique: the way you speak, behave, dress, and respond to conflict to reflect a majority White environment.*
>
> *It means becoming a chameleon in many ways. You behave one way at work, then relax around family or friends, knowing you'll be free from judgment there. I learned this at a young age. Sadly, in many ways, that agility led to my professional success.*
>
> *These types of adaptability skills and my ability to maintain constant internal vigilance allowed me to fit in at social events and even to identify corporate-culture*

> *norms. I don't have the luxury to sit awkwardly on the sidelines or even indulge in talking to other BIPOC (Black, indigenous, and other people of color) for extensive periods of time without scrutiny. I have to work the room, so people are comfortable with my otherness. Fortunately, as an extrovert, some of this comes easy for me. But it's also exhausting.*

I sang in church and in school music programs as a child. To make extra money for the family, I entered talent shows. I lucked out when I discovered a talent show on Monday nights at a bar called The Crazy Horse Saloon. The first prize was $75. I decided on the spot that I was going to win that money. I told my mom what I wanted to do and made her sign me up. Next, I used my savings to buy some new sheet music and begged my music teacher to help me rehearse after school.

The song was one of my mother's favorites: "Betcha By Golly Wow" by the Stylistics. I calculated that the audience would have old people like my mother (early thirties seemed old to my juvenile mind) and that they would like my song selection.

I carefully planned my outfit: a borrowed red silky blouse, black miniskirt, and my best pleather boots from Payless (sexy, but age appropriate for a thirteen-year-old, I thought). The evening arrived. I begged for some lipstick, marched myself onto that stage, and belted out that song. I used my practiced dramatic hand gestures, blew kisses to the audience, and told the host it was my dream to win.

And guess what? All my planning paid off. I won! *Well, hell,* I thought. *This is doable.*

I then went on to win for the next six consecutive weeks. I loved the applause and hugs from my family, and my name was even announced on our local radio station. I was proud to give my mom money for groceries, and we even got Chinese takeout to celebrate my wins. Not so bad for ten minutes on a stage!

> *Lesson learned: taking the initiative can result in making money, and planning allows you to win.*

This was one of the first times when I had a sense of being able to control my destiny, even if just for a little bit. It may not sound like that big of a deal, but it significantly shifted a number of things between my mother and me. I was intent that my plan would work, but she had doubts. As I kept winning, I gave her the prize money. The next weekend we would go, and I would win again. I began to notice that each time I handed her the envelope, she seemed torn between being proud of me and definitely a little weirded out.

She probably was thinking, *Who ARE you?* I was very different from my mom, and I continued to be even more different throughout her life. If I put my mind to accomplishing a goal, I would doggedly remove obstacles until I achieved it. I was such an intense and purposeful child, and we had such different personalities.

Those talent shows created a little bit of a shift in our relationship—probably earlier than the ones most girls have with their parents. I realized I had a distinct survivor instinct. I knew that I would and could do whatever it took to get what I wanted. I would not be deterred. This would later serve me well both in college and on the job. I never had a defeatist or quitter attitude. I felt I could achieve whatever I set my mind to. Later on, I realized that attitude is even more important than aptitude. Life is mental meaning; you win or lose at things based on your mindset.

When I was a child, the adults around me would often say that I acted very "grown." I did boss my mom and brother around. I had things that needed to be done and places to go, and I hated procrastination. I had and still have a personality that is very rule bound and structured. I understand that having a sense of control was one of my coping mechanisms because I didn't always feel taken care of or safe. Plus, I worried about my mom's capabilities.

I know I drove my mother crazy with my insistence that things needed to be done in a specific way and as soon as possible She couldn't have had a more Type A child. I was impatient and demanding in a way that ran very contrary to both her and my brother's laid-back personalities. I have to give her credit now, even if I wasn't mature enough to know it then. She was so patient and accepting of this strange child who was so different from her.

I remember that it bothered me that my mother kept a messy, disorganized house. Once, I organized all of her clothes in her closet because some items were hanging haphazardly on hangers while others lay in piles on the floor. I kept the clothes she wore most often, and everything else I bagged up for Goodwill pick-up. She discovered my organization project just in time before those much-needed clothes were accepted as a donation.

My mother was uncharacteristically angry with me and insisted that I had no authority over how she organized or did not organize her clothing. She so rarely got angry with me that I realized immediately I'd crossed a line. I'd disrespected her boundaries—also something common in children who grow up as I did. Learning to recognize and respect other people's boundaries and to set my own was a huge turning point.

Understanding that I needed to accept people's idiosyncrasies and imperfections, respect their boundaries, and acknowledge my own was something I developed somewhat later in life. One of my biggest struggles is dealing with my impatience with people, processes, and ignorance.

> *As a young girl watching my mother manage her life, I was determined to have a different one. In some ways I did, and yet in other ways, I emulated her life. For most of our lives we operate on the subconscious level, and most of our interactions are directed by subconscious programming. Our parents or caregivers directly or indirectly program our brains when we're young. Like*

it or not, we adopt some of our parents' behaviors and personalities.

I realize now that when I was young, I was often fighting against a deep sense of shame. I was driven because I wanted to have a different life for myself, my mother, and my brother. I wanted my home to look perfect and clean. I remember feeling embarrassed going to supermarkets and wanting things that I couldn't have. I was disappointed that I would frequently miss birthday parties because I knew I didn't have money for a gift. My solution was to take well-planned risks that could result in a financial gain, and I wanted to continue on that path.

Despite our different personalities, my mother and I were very close. She, my brother, and I formed a trio and rarely were apart from each other except while at school or work. My mother had a talent for making the ordinary special. She would arrange deviled eggs, cheese and crackers, and fruit attractively on a quilt that she spread in the yard so we could have spontaneous picnics. We would lie next to each other, my mother and me reading and my brother playing with a toy, for hours.

My mother was diagnosed with lung cancer in her later years. She came to live with me for her last year of life. She died young, at seventy. She passed on at home with my brother and me holding her hands—the three of us together one last time.

My mother's funeral service was standing room only, attended by many family members, friends, former coworkers, and church members who talked about her kind acts and great cooking. Through the years, people would bring plastic containers to my mother's house in the hopes they could take home leftovers of potato salad, ribs, or fried chicken from her delicious meals.

At her funeral we played all of her favorite gospel songs and the room smelled sweet from all the flowers. I miss her every day.

CHAPTER 3

Dad - Oh Yes, I Have Daddy Issues

"I am so fast that last night I turned off the light switch in my hotel room and was in bed before the room was dark." ~ **Muhammad Ali**

Chapter Soundtrack: "That's the Way of the World" ~ Earth, Wind & Fire, 1974

If there was ever a person who lived by his own rules, it was my dad. His becoming a police officer after the Vietnam War is extremely ironic. The traits that got him into trouble were the same traits that made him so popular.

He was a complex man: hot-tempered, loving, narcissistic, and extroverted. I have memories of spontaneous house parties during the weekends we spent with him. He would start frying chicken while Earth, Wind & Fire blasted on the stereo, and people would start showing up. The guests might be other police officers, neighbors, family, or members of a motorcycle club (gang) he knew.

The house would be full of his "friends," while a smoky haze of marijuana and record album covers with lines of cocaine served as the backdrop. I see this as the start of my ability to navigate chaos and survive despite extreme circumstances and conflicting values at play in front of me.

How did I manage as a young child? Well, I did so in a variety of ways. My father would frequently forget about my brother and me. I would gather blankets and make tents for Robbie and me in the back of Dad's cargo van, away from the people and the noise. We would also hide in his bedroom closet with food and fall asleep where we felt safe. Despite knowing this was bad behavior on our father's part, we would rarely tell my mom because we still wanted to spend time with him.

I knew how to be a mini hostess at these parties. At around nine years old, I became an expert at rolling joints. I would carefully remove the hard stems and seeds so each joint would be perfect. My dad would brag about my skills, and his friends would give me their dime bags and papers to roll joints for them. Talk about a strange form of dysfunctional child labor! Sometimes his buddies would give me money, which I would hide from my dad.

Another memory I have is of going to a summer concert with my dad and brother. It was an all-day event in a park. It was very hot, and my brother and I fell asleep under a tree at some point. When we woke up, my father was not to be found. We wandered around for a long while and finally saw a familiar group of people.

My dad's friend Tommy was a member of the Wheels of Souls motorcycle club. This "club" had and still has a reputation for drugs and violence. I have no idea why my father had these friends, but I was happy to see familiar faces. I ran up to Tommy and said in a voice shaky from crying, "I can't find my dad!"

Tommy was a heavily tattooed, light-skinned Black man who was wearing a black leather vest (despite the summer heat) with chains and spikes. He squatted down next to me and gently asked, "What's up, baby girl?" He added, "I think your dad left." He could clearly see that my brother and I were upset.

So the next thing I knew, I had a too-big helmet on my head and my brother and I were on the backs of motorcycles, heading to my father's apartment. When we arrived, my dad was sitting on his patio, clearly high. He smiled at my brother and me like nothing was wrong. Tommy just shook his head.

My dad's girlfriend, Connie, left briefly and returned with hot dogs for my brother and me. She made sure we were eating, then she left. I felt mad and defeated. My brother was very quiet. I snuck into the bedroom and called my mom. I told her I felt sick and wanted to come home. She agreed to come get us, and when she arrived, I said I had a stomachache. My father waved goodbye.

We didn't tell my mother what had happened. Even at nine years old I knew that what had taken place was very bad. Still, I didn't want my mom to argue with my father.

> *It's not uncommon for children of parents who abuse drugs to also succumb to addictions. I have no idea why my response to this type of exposure didn't lead me down that path. I remember thinking that this is what adults do, and the craziness I witnessed provided a cautionary tale.*

My father came from a large family that was very loving toward my mother, brother, and me. His father (John) was a retired police officer, as was his eldest brother (John Jr.). He had three other siblings—two sisters and another brother (Valeria, Rose, and Kenny). We all often spent holidays together. At times I felt they were compensating for my dad's behavior. They loved my father despite his shortcomings and wished he could be a better parent. Unfortunately, it was a tolerance I didn't possess.

Other memories from weekends with Dad included his revolving door of girlfriends. Of course, I despised them because they took his attention from me. One was Joy. I would torment her and insist that she sit in the back seat of the car so I could sit up front with my dad. He enjoyed my tantrums for his attention and would weaponize my childish jealousy to keep his girlfriends on edge. I cringe now when I think about my behavior.

> *Verbal abuse is a learned behavior. The human brain is highly adaptable. Born into a safe, nurturing environment, a child's brain develops normally; when born into one that is either unsupported or hostile, the brain does not.*

There was also Anna, who lived with my dad when I was eleven and twelve years old. She was only twenty or twenty-one herself, and she was like a big sister. Unlike my father's previous girlfriends, she paid attention to me, taught me about makeup, and bought me clothes at the mall. I would follow her around like a puppy, impulsively hugging her and having deep conversations about boys I liked at school. This drove my father nuts because he was not the focus of our attention. The shoe was on the other foot for once!

One day, my father took me on a run. (He would do this occasionally to help combat my "chubbiness," as he liked to call it.) While we ran that early morning, he asked if I knew the difference between heterosexuality and homosexuality. Puzzled, I asked why he was asking me about this. He then proceeded to tell me that my behavior toward Anna made him think I must be gay. His tone was stern and clearly he was disappointed in me.

I didn't know how to process this, and I remember feeling dirty and bad. When we returned home, Anna asked me if I wanted to help make breakfast with her and my brother. I said, "No," and immediately went to my room.

I was very subdued when I returned to my mom's house that Sunday evening. My mom asked me repeatedly what was wrong, and I finally shared the conversation I'd had with my dad. My mom teared up and said, "Barbara, you're not to feel bad about the way you do about Anna. It's completely natural to care about someone who's so nice to you."

I was reassured by this, but from that point forward I was so self-conscious around Anna that our relationship became very distant. My father was pleased and seemed to pay me more attention when I visited him.

My father exhibited a great deal of controlling and narcissistic behavior. He also disciplined us by beating us with a belt, or he would smack me across the mouth with his hand if he felt I was speaking disrespectfully to him. I spent a lot of time trying to anticipate his moods, as he was very mercurial from one visit to the next.

> *How women mold themselves to please men is a theme I see with my own daughters and friends. And it starts young. Our fathers teach us many lessons that lodge themselves in our self-conscious minds. These lessons determine whether we see ourselves as attractive or smart, tell us when it's okay for us to speak, and even direct how we interact with other women.*
>
> *Our self-image is linked to our fathers' opinions of us. For example, did they constantly critique our appearance or our weight? This shows up in the workplace*

> *for many of us, male and female. Are we hypervigilant about others' opinions? Do we seek to avoid conflict or want to be liked? Be mindful of how your past influences how you show up at work or in other relationships.*

My dad also had qualities I admired. He was courageous, and he received merit awards for bravery as a police officer for putting himself in harm's way to save others. I remember seeing him in his patrolman's uniform with his badge, hat, and shiny shoes, and thinking how amazing he was. He later became a detective and solved dozens of cases.

He was always meticulous, orderly, and neat. I immediately knew something was wrong if his personal appearance, car, or home seemed uncared for. My father also had a rare ability to charm people and keep the attention of an audience. He could recount a story, even one that others had heard before, and have everyone belly laughing. He was quirky; he often answered the phone with "County Morgue" or "My name is Jimmy; I'll take anything you gimme."

Although women were drawn to my dad's good looks and personality, he also had many male friends who loved to be around him—to play basketball, listen to music, or just party. He seemed happier when he had lots of people around.

Undoubtedly, I see parallels between my father and my own extroverted personality, my love of music, and my sense of humor. My father had a fearlessness and a boldness that I admired, and I'm flattered when family members see it in me.

Unfortunately, my father's addictions led him to violent and impulsive behavior. His temper was explosive at times. This led to other dramatic events. My mother eventually remarried, and my father didn't like my stepfather. My teenage brother, who had never shared my mother's attention with or taken parental direction from another man, struggled with this new family construct. I didn't like my stepfather either, but I was away from home by that time, so I had fewer interactions with him.

My stepfather thought of himself as a disciplinarian, and my brother often complained to my father about his unhappiness. After one particularly tense argument, my stepfather hit my brother. My father showed up at the house, and a fight between him and my stepfather ensued. My father, who was at that time retired from the police force, always carried his gun with him.

As the story goes, my father had a crowbar in tow as well as his gun on that visit. He told my stepfather to choose which one he should use, since he'd heard that my stepfather liked to beat up on boys less than half his size. Needless to say, my father gave my stepfather what he believed was a lesson. My stepfather pressed charges and my father was ultimately sent to prison for attacking my stepfather while in possession of a gun.

I was a junior in college when all this happened. Although I was estranged from my father at the time, I was conflicted by my loyalty to my brother, who my father believed he was defending. Even though I was only twenty years old, my father gave me access to manage his banking and pension payments while he was in prison.

I visited him monthly, taking him food and toiletries. I was worried and anxious that other inmates might harm an ex-police officer. When I visited him, I told my college roommates and friends that I was going home for the weekend because I was ashamed about where I was really going. Having a parent in prison wasn't something I wanted to share. My father spent nearly three years in prison and was released early for good behavior.

If you're thinking a stint in prison is the end of the story, you're wrong. After prison, my father returned home and, for reasons I don't fully understand, slipped back into his addiction. Sadly, he progressed to smoking crack cocaine. I remember very clearly sitting in my office at a major trade association when he called. "BP," he said, "you gotta come and get me or I'm going to be dead in a week." I left work early, saying I had a sudden headache. I was twenty-three years old.

I called rehab facilities in the D.C. area. I found a thirty-day program in Fairfax, Virginia, that would take his police retirement benefits. I drove to New Jersey to get him. My father was living at the house that belonged to my grandfather. The house was dirty and empty of furniture, and he was sitting on a mattress on the floor. He looked up at me with vacant eyes, mumbling, "You came to get me?"

At that stage of his life, my father was a six-foot-one skeleton. His clothing was dirty and hung off his body. We drove to a local K-Mart to shop, as he had no possessions except his wallet. I purchased pants, pajamas, a few shirts, and some toiletries. We then went to purchase some shoes, and he mustered up enough energy to indignantly ask me, "How can I walk around in cheap K-Mart brand sneakers?" I told him, "That's what I can afford, so you're going to have to tough it out."

The stark reality was that I was spending my rent money, and he was complaining he wasn't getting Nike or Adidas sneakers. I drove back to Alexandria, Virginia, where I was living, with him sleeping the entire time in the back seat. I would glance back, shocked at how frail he was. He looked helpless. When we arrived, I insisted that he shower, and I made him a sandwich. He promptly said it was a "dry-ass sandwich," to which I replied, "At least it's free." For some reason, we both started laughing. The next morning, I dropped him off at the rehab center.

I then drove to my office, poured myself a cup of coffee, and thanked my work colleagues who inquired about my headache. I had become very good at compartmentalizing my life. I knew instinctively that sharing that I had a drug-addicted father wasn't going to reflect well upon me at work. I believed I had to present a specific image to be successful. I didn't want people to believe that my life included all the negative stereotypes about Black people that people saw every evening on TV.

I knew that my coworkers or boss could potentially judge me even though my father's actions weren't my own. My every absence would be scrutinized, and concerns about my stability might suddenly arise. Working in HR, I'd seen it happen to others, and I knew that it could derail professional progress. People assume that your life mirrors theirs, and while some might be empathetic when they discover it doesn't, many are not.

The rehab stay seemed to stabilize my father. Fortunately, he had his pension, which he supplemented with assorted jobs. He ultimately owned a fish market, then worked in sales until poor health kept him home. He died of lung cancer at age seventy. His funeral was well attended. People told stories of his epic parties, his sense of humor, his fearless personality, and especially his unrealized potential.

> *Like many children of parents who suffered from drug addiction, I learned to hide or ignore pain, rejection, and even anger. I was clearly designated as a caregiver for my father. The role I played is called the "Hero."*
>
> *Classically, the Hero strives to balance out the negativity and shame surrounding addiction in the family. The Hero is high achieving, a perfectionist that values order and control. Often the firstborn child, the Hero assumes many parental responsibilities, possibly even serving as a surrogate parent to their own siblings. The*

> *Hero may become a highly motivated leader, excelling in school or in their career. On the downside of the equation, however, they may battle extreme stress and be unable to relinquish control.*[VIII] ~

My favorite husband (my second one) never met my father, but he has heard many larger-than-life stories about him over the years. Last year, we were having a conversation after a family gathering that members of my father's side of the family had attended.

My husband said to me, "The more I hear about your dad, the more I learn. I used to see so much of your mom in you. You've very much a caregiver, and being a mom is so important to you. You like to take care of everyone like she did her best to do. But there are these entrepreneurial, risk-taker, extroverted parts of you that clearly are your dad. He had so much unrealized potential; there's a lot of you that I can see was influenced by him, whether it's genetic or not."

That prompted me to write more about my dad because he was a deeply flawed person who didn't quite know how to love me or be a father. A Black man in this country has to combat so many obstacles and many share his struggles. But my father did have a significant impact on my empathetic perspective and my ability to understand the damage that one can do to themselves. It's a cautionary tale to me, and I'm still learning and understanding the impact my father's choices and decisions had on my brother and me.

CHAPTER 4

Grandparents

"Love is an action, never simply a feeling." ~ **bell hooks**

Chapter Soundtrack: "What a Wonderful World" ~ Louis Armstrong, 1967

My maternal grandparents, Anna Mae and Leo, were the support system and stable foundation for our family. To say they made a huge impact on my life is an understatement. They met when my grandmother was twenty-nine and my grandfather was twenty-three. Yup. She was a cougar. All of the grandchildren called them Mom Mom and Pop Pop. My kids, for some reason, called them Old Grandma and Old Pop Pop.

Anna Mae was born in 1917 and grew up in the small town of Milton, Florida. She had three sisters and three brothers. She was a very talented seamstress and a wonderful cook. She made dresses for her daughters and hemmed and tailored pants for the men. She was stubborn and had a temper. We knew that if we broke a rule at her house or sassed her, she was going to get a switch from the bush by the driveway and she was going to get us!

I also have memories of sitting between her legs as she combed, brushed, and braided my hair into ponytails. Her fingers smelled of garlic, onions, or mint, as she was always cooking in her kitchen.

She would share memories of growing up in the South and the racism she'd suffered. One of her brothers was lynched as a young man, and she would tear up when sharing this story, every time.

> *Generational trauma is real, particularly in Black families, who share the history of their family's struggle, loss, and experiences with racism. Part of the reason this is done is certainly to preserve history, but also to provide a cautionary tale because institutional racism still exists. You teach your Black son or grandson tactics to employ while driving and getting pulled over by the police because you want him to be prepared to deal with any situation—because his life could be on the line.*

My grandmother had two children from a former relationship and went on to have three daughters with her second husband. She was a housecleaner until well into her fifties, working primarily for a client who fortunately paid her legally and deducted Social Security and Medicare taxes so she could later claim those benefits.

Anna Mae was quirky, and she was a boss. She was always very nicely dressed and smelled like lavender. She wore bright lipstick, and her favorite color was purple. She ran her house very precisely, washing and waxing the kitchen floor on Saturdays. She cooked every holiday dinner from scratch, and we celebrated our birthdays at her house. She would bake all of the grandchildren's birthday cakes every year. She never learned to drive. I remember taking the bus with her to go places. If a bus wasn't convenient, she would call one of her children to take her somewhere—and they did!

One of my recollections about my grandmother was her quilting expertise. She would gather all kinds of fabric in bags near her sewing machine. She often had several quilts in varying stages of completion lying around. Her quilts could be found folded at the end of every family member's bed, and old ones were used for picnics. Her quilts were traditional nine-patch or pinwheel patterns that she learned from her mother.

Getting a quilt or even a jar of her delicious, spiced pear preserves wasn't a given. She would keep track of who she deemed was treating her with the respect she deserved or was living right by God. She wielded a great deal of influence in the family but balanced her sometimes quick temper with kindness.

My grandfather was born in 1923 and grew up in Orange, New Jersey. He had one brother. His father was a street cleaner and his mother was a maid. When his parents got older, he purchased the plot of land next to him so they could leave city life, and they built a house next door. Leo served as a cook in the navy during World War II and later worked at a foundry, retiring as a supervisor. After that he worked as a driver for his former employer's wife to make extra money.

> *"Success is to be measured not so much by the position that one has reached in life as by the obstacles which he has overcome while trying to succeed."* ~ **Booker T. Washington**

Leo was a very patient man, kind and quite religious. He was notoriously cheap and drove old cars. I remember him mending his socks when they had holes in them. He loved being a "girl dad," and all of his grandchildren loved to spend time with him. He listened to me very intently when I babbled on about some topic I felt passionately about, then he'd offer his feedback. He was so intelligent. He loved to read, and I wish he'd had the same opportunities as a young adult that I had.

Here's an odd story about my grandfather. In his late seventies he was diagnosed with throat cancer and was hospitalized for surgery. Like many Black people, he didn't trust doctors and was convinced he might die. Prior to his surgery date, he took me to a local attorney to update his will, and he made me the executor of his modest estate. While he was in the hospital, my grandmother decided to refresh the bedroom and, while moving the bed, she discovered a large lump under the carpet. It was $2,000 in a plastic bag!

While visiting my grandfather, I told him about the discovery that had been made, and he asked me if anyone had looked behind the dresser. I assured him that no one had, and he was very relieved. Apparently, he had another stash that was safe from my grandmother's sharp eyes. When anyone in the family had a financial crisis, my grandfather would often help them. Once I'd learned about his personal banking method, it was our little secret.

> *"Love is the absence of judgment."*
> ~ **The Dalai Lama**

I was fortunate to have unconditional love and support from my grandparents, who seemed to instinctively know I needed them to be my familial cheerleaders. They went to school events, openly expressed their pride in my accomplishments, and gave me a safe place to just be. My grandmother had only an elementary school education, so to see her eldest grandchild demonstrate academic success was a validation of the sacrifices both she and my grandfather made for their family.

My grandparents went to church every Sunday, usually accompanied by most of the family. My grandfather would wear a suit, his good shoes, and sometimes a hat with a feather in it. My grandmother had dresses and suits with matching hats and shoes! I liked to sit with them because she gave me mints so I would be quiet and let me fan myself if it was hot. When church inevitably went longer than an hour, my brother and I would get sleepy. She would put her arm around us, and I would lay my head on her soft chest.

I remember my great-grandmother would always stand up and request her favorite gospel songs, "Sweet Hour of Prayer" and "Jesus Is on the Main Line," then sway to the piano and everyone's voices. After church, we would all gather at my grandparents' home for a late breakfast. It is one of my fondest memories.

My grandmother would serve her homemade biscuits with butter and preserves, and my grandfather would fry eggs, bacon, and sausages. My cousins and I would exchange our church clothes for play clothes and disappear into the woods behind their house for hours. I also remember having so much fun with my great-grandparents, who lived next door, and my uncle, who lived across the street.

> *Spirituality and family traditions are especially important in building a sense of self and a connection to a higher power. This has been so key for me. The concept of faith or believing in what I can't see and understanding that I'm not in control have become a lifelong meditation theme.*

I was also fortunate to grow up with my great-grandparents, as they lived next door to my grandparents. My Great-Grandfather Willie was legally blind and wore a hearing aid. I have vivid memories of him. He wore corduroy pants in the summertime, which puzzled me because there was never a bead of sweat on him. He also chewed tobacco and spit into an old coffee can he kept by his side. My Great-Grandmother Anna was a thin, wiry woman and the most unselfish person I knew. She would have special food just for us grandkids: Nabisco chocolate chip cookies, Little Debbie pecan rolls, and Ellio's pizza.

Their little house was a safe harbor for me. I often spent the night with them. Watching TV on their black-and-white set while cuddled on the couch next to my great-grandmother is one of my fondest memories. Later she got a color TV, and my brother and I would bicker over watching *The Six Million Dollar Man* or *The Sonny and Cher Show*.

My great-grandmother paid my mother's rent for her first apartment after the divorce. What she had to sacrifice to do this I can't imagine. When my great-grandfather died, there, in the trunk at the end of his bed, was a stash of cash—neatly sorted ones, fives, tens and twenties. Having lived through the Great Depression, he still feared banks. Even my great-grandmother was shocked!

While my children have solid memories of their grandparents, they didn't have the robust multigenerational experiences that I was so fortunate to grow up with. My grandparents and great-grandparents lived through extreme poverty, racism, and segregation, yet they had such optimism about life and maintained their humanity.

The grace, wisdom, and self-sacrifice they showed toward their family is an example I can only hope to emulate.

Family is so important to me. It informs how I parent, lead, and walk through life. It is this connection to my past and my memories of struggle and an insistence on fairness and empathy that will often lead me to a professional decision or judgment. In fact, my identity and sense of self are derived from family legacies—the work ethic I saw and the sense of collective survival I experienced.

CHAPTER 5

Brother

The greatest gift our parents ever gave us was each other.

Chapter Soundtrack: "Lean on Me" ~ Bill Withers, 1972

My brother, Robbie, is one of my favorite people in the world. Although we're three years apart, we're very close, and I definitely treat him to this day as my baby brother. Laid back and good natured, he certainly has been quieter than me from the start. Our family stories recount that Robbie barely talked until he was four years old. I acted as his translator.

"Robbie wants a hot dog," I would state. Puzzled by this, adults would turn to Robbie and ask him, "Do you want a hot dog?" To their great frustration, he would quietly nod and point to me. My mother often said that when Robbie was born, I claimed he was my baby, and "that was that." I was both his protector and friend. We were inseparable, and I hope my children are able to sustain the same kind of life-long bond with each other.

Our closeness and bond were, I believe, partly fate and partly a survival tactic. He may have been too young to understand what was going on at times during our chaotic childhood, particularly when visiting with our father. But he knew who to trust. I, too, knew his loyalty to me was unwavering.

While close to my mother, Robbie was very tethered to my father. Often our father would say he was going to pick us up but never arrive. Robbie, however, would sit calmly waiting, peeking out the window and hoping far past my ability to believe Dad would arrive.

My father was very gentle and affectionate with Robbie. I don't recall my brother receiving many harsh words or much discipline. In fact, that love was something my dad and I had in common. We both loved Robbie and appreciated his easygoing, good-natured personality. Robbie was very forgiving of my dad's behavior, while I would be mad. He would say, "He doesn't mean it. He'll change."

As I was writing this book, I read portions to Robbie, and when I reached the section about my singing in the talent shows, it triggered a specific memory for him. He said, "Oh! That's when we would get French onion soup!" That's all he remembers. He was quite young at the time, and we didn't have that much money, so being able to go to that nightclub was a rare treat.

When I was performing, they would give the singers' guests freebies—French onion soup or some type of appetizer. So to my brother as a little boy, that fancy bowl of French onion soup made those outings special. He doesn't really recollect much of what I was doing. He just remembers getting kind of dressed up and being able to stay up late—and that he got this soup that was like nothing we would have gotten at home.

From his perspective, the biggest deal was that we were going out somewhere fancy and eating unusually good food. He didn't actually connect it with what I was doing to make it possible!

It's appropriate that it's primarily the food that he recalled from that time. Ultimately becoming a chef, Robbie is the foodie of the family. Cooking is his creative outlet. Ironically, a chaotic, fast-paced kitchen isn't intimidating in the least to him. He loves cookbooks and has a refined palate. He has saved me from my cooking mistakes over and over. He doesn't have to stand up on a stage to shine. His food speaks for itself.

To this day Robbie and I speak to each other about our problems and fears. He's a peacekeeper, like our mother. And perhaps because of our childhood, he treasures harmony and routine. He's an extraordinary brother and uncle—loyal, patient, and caring toward me and my children always. With both our parents gone, we profoundly realize our connection. We're survivors bound by our childhood—both good and bad. Best of all, he still tolerates my big-sister attitude as he enters his fifties.

Robbie is happily married to a wonderful woman named Kesone. She's from Laos and is a devout Buddhist. My brother has very happily become part of her large extended family. Out of respect for her family, my brother shaved his head and eyebrows when her father died. He was cleansed and sat with the monks for hours praying in the temple.

While attending the funeral, I looked at my brother sitting there calmly in his borrowed robes, showing love for his wife's family in his typical quiet way. This is what makes him special.

CHAPTER 6

Life Away from Home

"The only person you are destined to become is the person you decide to be." ~ **Ralph Waldo Emerson**

Chapter Soundtrack: "Candy Girl" ~ New Edition, 1982

One of my mom's good friends sent her son to a private boarding school in Pennsylvania. He and I had been classmates since elementary school, so I was curious about where he went. It was a boarding school for "poor" children. The school also offered financial support for college, so it could open doors for me to actually attend a university.

Milton and Catherine Hershey founded the Milton Hershey School in 1909 with money they earned from the Hershey chocolate company. The Hersheys established a state-chartered trust, now valued at approximately $17 billion, to support the school with the profits from Hershey companies. Every time you buy a Hershey chocolate bar, look at the label. The proceeds from the sale of the candy supports the Milton Hershey School.

After much discussion, my mother made an appointment for my brother and me to visit and interview at the Milton Hershey School. I remember riding in our car up to the impressive domed building called Founders Hall to speak with an admissions person. I thought, *I can go here. It's so pretty and clean and fancy.* I was ultimately accepted, but my little brother didn't want to leave home. I worried about leaving my mom and brother on their own, but I knew I wanted to try a different path.

Ambition means sacrifice and risk-taking, leaning into fear, and openness to change.

A few months later, with only a suitcase in tow, I arrived back on campus and moved into a large house with thirteen other teenage girls and a set of house parents. I shared a decent-sized room with another new girl. She was petite, very fair, and blonde, and we both were wondering what to expect from our rooming assignment. I remember I had tiny cornrows with gold beads that click-clacked when I moved my head. That hairstyle was a mistake. It made me stand out and look different. The other Black girls noticed and didn't like it. Although I didn't intend to be a show-off, the others perceived me that way. More on that later.

Our house parents gave us a tour and told us about expectations and chores. I wasn't worried. I liked rules, and expectations didn't bother me. But that all changed when we walked outside to the barn. Apparently, I'd missed the part during the admissions discussion when milking cows was discussed.

The barn smelled of hay, silage (food for the cows), and cow manure—lots of manure. The school wanted to instill a strong work ethic, so there were small dairy operations at some student homes, and students performed many of the activities necessary to run it.

Living away from home at a young age is jarring and living with lots of people is a recipe for all kinds of drama. Living with thirteen other teenage girls who were all trying to figure out who they were was exhausting. Although we all had to follow a similar routine and schedule, everyone processes things differently. The typical daily schedule included half the girls working in the barn, milking cows, and taking care of other dairy farm duties. The other half cooked breakfast, did laundry, cleaned common areas, and did minor yard work.

All of this started at six in the morning, seven days a week. Let's start with the fact that I'm a germaphobe, so being around animals that smelled and lots of other natural foul substances was not to my liking. When the rotation switched to household duties, I was infinitely happier.

The girls added a degree of complexity to my life, particularly as some had been at the school since kindergarten and had allegiances and bonds that were impenetrable to the new girls. Some of the established girls were bullies who felt it was their duty to haze the newbies. Girls typically didn't indulge in physical hazing; that was left to the boys. Instead, girls engaged in psychological warfare. Why is it that women can very easily figure out your insecurities, whether it be weight, hair, or the internal blemishes invisible to the human eye?

Initially, my strategy was to get everyone to like me, so I let people borrow clothes, hair bows, and albums. But I discovered that some just kept the borrowed items and took advantage of my need for friendship. I had a large plastic case of colored beads that I would use to decorate my braids. Many of the girls had braids too, but not the beads to decorate the ends. In less than two months, either by theft or "borrowing," I was left with none.

Girls I didn't even know from other student homes were wearing the beads and wouldn't admit to how they'd received them. I spoke with one of my aunts on the phone, and she told me the following: "Stop trying to be nice. They're confusing that with weakness." My mom later sent me a new supply of beads (they were very inexpensive). I hid them in my room and told anyone who asked to borrow them that I didn't have enough to share.

Some of my false friends promptly rejected me, but others seemed unbothered by the new Barbara with boundaries. It's important to let people earn your generosity and trust. Don't give it away too easily. This was a valuable lesson to me about human nature: you can't control what others do, but you can control your actions and responses to what they do to you. There is power in this, and you need to claim this—particularly in the workplace.

> *According to Wikipedia (no snarky comments, please): "Personal boundaries are guidelines, rules, or limits that a person creates to identify reasonable, safe, and permissible ways for other people to behave towards them and how they will respond when someone passes those limits."* [ix]

Living in a communal environment, you learn to become hypervigilant about everyone's moods and disputes, as well as opportunities to build your own brand. It's the age-old dilemma of, Is it better to be feared or loved? I leaned toward loved, but occasionally I had to stand up for myself or learn to build allies.

There was still the false narrative from some of my Black classmates that wanting to excel academically was "acting too White." I later mentored young Black children and would always emphasize that academic achievement shouldn't be associated with race. Moreover, no one should diminish or limit what their intellectual ability could be. I'm deeply saddened to acknowledge the self-defeating narrative that exists in the Black community. So many of us don't know how high to aspire and never have the opportunity to do so.

Alternatively, some of my White classmates and teachers held me to a standard that was often hard to maintain. At times, they almost seemed to be waiting for me to exemplify some stereotypical characteristic that they could point to and label. For example, I kept being encouraged to play basketball when I had neither the skill nor the desire for the game. My lack of interest in the sport perplexed my White classmates to no end. For the record, I'm not a good dancer, either.

However, I was beyond letting those standards distract me. I had goals for myself that I was singularly focused on. What helped me thrive at Hershey, however, was an innate understanding that everyone had baggage. Whether it was poverty, being an orphan, or having family members who struggled with addictions—we all had issues we were dealing with.

I was extremely fortunate and grateful that my mother visited me regularly, along with other family members, and we spoke weekly by phone. Having a parent who cared and with whom I had a connection was far more than many other kids had.

I thrived at the school, enjoying the small class sizes and exposure to a broader world outside my small town in New Jersey. To say I was active would be an understatement. My high school yearbook noted that I was involved in Girl's Chorus, New Horizons (a jazz singing group), Cross Country, Track, Softball manager, Swimming manager, Student Cabinet, Student Leadership Society, Officials Post, Peer Group Counseling, and Student Home Council.

These clubs, teams, and leadership roles built my confidence in my ability to engage and interact with people of any age, ethnicity, and socioeconomic status. I look back on this time and understand that my emotional intelligence and intuition about people was a key skill for me—one I would later rely on in my professional career.

I took part in as many activities as I could and felt that there was definitely support for me to have a successful life. The internal drumbeat in my head pushed me. The beat said, "Keep it moving, girl. You have no Plan B."

My time at Hershey wasn't just "my time at Hershey." It was a type of training ground. I learned the basic skills I would build on and use to this day. When I encounter work challenges, I seek to leverage all of my colleagues' strengths, ask the tough questions, and give praise or a kind word as appropriate. I still model the behavior I saw and experienced at the Milton Hershey School. I had many opportunities to refine those skills at an early age. Attending the school changed my trajectory. It made my dreams of going to college a possibility.

One of the things I stress to my children and those young adults I coach, and mentor is to never see challenges and hard times as bad luck or misfortune, but as lessons in disguise. Learn from them. Grow from them and put the things you learn into use in your professional and personal lives. Everything happens for a reason, and if you look for that silver lining, you'll find it. You may not find it immediately, but never stop looking.

Ultimately, attending the Milton Hershey School led me to college, and the school helped fund my education. More on the school later, but ultimately as an adult, I found my way back to Hershey to try to give back what I had gained as a child. I am a part of an active collective alumni family whose shared experiences create unique bonds. I graduated high school on a beautiful day in June and went on to attend Rutgers University in New Jersey.

PART 2

Adult Problems and Adult Games = Lessons Learned

CHAPTER 7

Stories of College Life

"The beautiful thing about learning is that no one can take it away from you." ~ **B. B. King**

Chapter Soundtrack: "Purple Rain" ~ Prince, 1984

Moving into my dorm room in a high-rise building was anticlimactic. Unlike most of my new college classmates, I'd already been living away from home. My mother and stepfather helped me move my boxes to my tiny, shared room. I had a very definitive decorating theme. I had the college dorm room starter set: a comforter with pink flowers, a pink rug, and pink and white towels for showers. I also had posters of Prince, George Michael, and Nelson Mandela. An interesting combo, huh?

As we walked around campus for a bit, I was not battling any pangs of homesickness. I was ready for my mom to leave so I could start my college life. I returned to my dorm room to catch my new roommate saying goodbye to her parents. I was excited to meet who I thought might be a new friend—a partner to eat with or accompany to parties. Those feelings of excitement were immediately squashed as she began to pack the clothes she had just put away. She said, "I'm going to live with my boyfriend off campus. You have the room to yourself."

I sat on my bed disappointed. I could hear other people laughing up and down the hallway. I felt like crying. I hadn't expected this situation. I needed a plan. So, I decided to wander around and introduce myself and meet other people.

I hate it when my best-laid plans don't go as I hope. There's nothing that frustrates a meticulous planner more than an unplanned circumstance.

Disappointment throughout your career is inevitable, and you must learn how to pivot. I've had technology failures, a critical person "no show," even wardrobe malfunctions. I've had an important presentation be poorly received and even a new boss who didn't like me. My personal favorite malfunction was the toilet paper attached to my shoe while I was walking into a board meeting. The point is, life is going to be full of disappointments—you have to solve for it and keep moving. There really isn't any other choice.

> *"When you find your path, you must not be afraid. You need to have sufficient courage to make mistakes. Disappointment, defeat, and despair are the tools God uses to show us the way." Brida,* ~ **Paulo Coelho**

The dorm was co-ed. So this was a big change to go from Milton Hershey to living with boys. All of the girls were decorating their rooms, showing off clothes, and talking about classes they were going to take. The boys' rooms were mostly unpacked, and they were playing Frisbee or kicking soccer balls down the hall. I gave myself an internal pep talk and knocked on the door closest to me.

Three girls were crammed into a room slightly larger than mine with a set of bunk beds and a twin bed. There was so much stuff that they were attempting to put away and organize it was laughable. "Hi, I'm Barbara," I said. "I'm next door and just found out I have a single." I laughed. One of the girls smiled and said, "How did you get a single?" The other girls stopped talking and motioned for me to come in and sit with them.

I told them the story and they all expressed disbelief. They said I should hang with them, and I offered them the use of one of my empty closets. Mission accomplished. At least initially, I would have some people to hang out with.

Rutgers University is a large institution. At the time it was a little over twenty thousand students. I was at the main campus, but there were multiple others to explore. Most of my classes were on my home campus, but I had a few at Douglass (all-girl college) and Livingston. I didn't have a car, so that meant taking buses.

It was intimidating to walk into lecture halls with three hundred students. I felt a bit lost. Fortunately, some of my classes had smaller class sizes, and I began to meet other students. I'm naturally outgoing, but I missed high school.

Fortunately, my three dorm friends and I began to have a friendship. We would meet for meals and explore the campus together. We didn't do everything together, however, because White students primarily ate together and partied together, as did the Black students. But I had made an important dorm connection and had the comfort of those relationships when I needed it.

If you observed what happened in campus dining halls, there were clearly patterns. If you had White roommates, occasionally you would eat with them, but most often you would eat with your Black friends. Like most college campuses in America, unless you attended a HBCU (Historically Black College or University), the Black students have to seek each other out.

I remember walking to class with a White friend, and every time I passed another Black student, we would speak and acknowledge each other. Invariably my White friends walking with me would say something like, "Barbara, you know everyone!" In a world where Black people are often not seen or acknowledged in a positive way, and on a campus where we were the minority, it mattered to us to greet, hug, and/or smile at other Black students. So, whether I knew them or not, there was an unspoken understanding of connectedness.

My social life started blossoming as I began to make more friends. For the first time in my life I had the opportunity to be in large, diverse student environments, clubs, classes, and parties. I felt validated and seen in a way I hadn't before as a student.

I worked for the school newspaper and protested against apartheid. Rutgers had South African investments, and students demanded that the university divest. I found I could passionately discuss the issues around apartheid, and I loved being part of collective protest. Although I already considered myself an independent person, college required lots of independent decision-making and presented a new set of healthy challenges for me.

I decided to be a political science major and enjoyed classroom debates. I had some amazing professors. Leveraging skills learned in high school, I understood the importance of building relationships. Even if I was getting good grades, I often met professors to get advice or make observations. This later led to me embracing networking and developing mutually beneficial relationships at work and throughout my career.

I had a friend who received a poor grade on an exam, and I encouraged her to speak with our professor. I accompanied her to the counseling appointment and helped explain her circumstance to the professor, whom I often had coffee with after class. To my friend's surprise, he was willing to give her an extra-credit assignment. Afterward, I explained to her the importance of building relationships with professors. It was hard for me to grasp why she didn't know this. I began to have an inkling of what my survival skills had taught me that others didn't know.

Through my newfound mentors I received valuable guidance that helped me throughout my time at college. As the first person in my family to attend college, I had no adult relative who could help me navigate the college experience. Building these relationships with professors and deans served me well later in life. When I relocated to Washington, D.C., after graduation, one of those deans introduced me to a colleague who helped me find my first job in the city.

> *First-generation college students have to juggle a lot as they navigate college because they don't have parents who can share their own college experiences. They don't have the support network, and they feel guilty asking their families for anything. As a low-income student, it can be challenging to fit in with students who have financial support from family. Traveling on weekends, participating in Greek life, and vacationing on spring break are often not possible. That doesn't mean first-generation students don't benefit as much as other students. They just benefit differently, often developing skills that will serve them better in the workforce than a regimen of intramural sports and parties does.*

I also had a work/study job at a study center for fifteen hours a week, from seven to ten on weeknights. After freshman year, I realized I needed more spending money.

One strategy was to take the money my scholarships provided for books and use some of it for new clothes. That meant I sometimes needed to borrow a book from a classmate, read it quickly, take notes, copy the critical passages, then return the book.

I found another job working at a local hotel as a hostess. Still an early riser, I worked from six in the morning to one in the afternoon. The hotel chef would let me make a sandwich to take with me, and I would rush to class after work ended. I look back on the schedule of a full-time student with two part-time jobs, and it seems implausible that I had time to study, have a social life, and juggle my secret responsibilities for my dad.

However, I learned that it's critical to schedule time and prioritize tasks. For the most part, I was comfortable saying no to anything that wasn't critical or didn't enhance my life. I was fortunate that I really enjoyed school and deep inside felt grateful to even be there. Those feelings fueled my inner hustle. I built critical time-management skills that served me later in life as I learned to juggle my jobs, classes, and social life.

I dated, but it was never anything serious until a friend introduced me to a tall, handsome, charismatic recent Rutgers graduate in my junior year. He drove a flashy sports car and had a reputation as a "player." And lots of my girlfriends had crushes on him. I was shocked by his interest in me, as I wasn't in his circle of friends. I was a bit of a nerd and was often teased about being so serious about my studies.

I also didn't do drugs, and, while I did drink socially, I wasn't a party girl. After my childhood, I had a deep fear of addiction of any type. My clothes weren't designer, and I drove an old car. I felt a bit intimidated by him, as I wasn't his normal type. My imposter syndrome was triggered big time while we were seeing each other.

We dated throughout the rest of my time in college. It was a tumultuous relationship. I now know through the benefits of therapy that I was attracted to the dysfunction I'd grown up with. I confused constant drama and relationship insecurity with love.

My college studies continued, and I contemplated going to law school or graduate school. My grandfather, whom I deeply respected, urged me to work and make money after graduation and to not take on student loans. He believed women should get married and have families. I absorbed his advice. I'm not sure that I fully understood the benefits of furthering my education or how or what to aspire to.

> *The will to win, the desire to succeed, the urge to reach your full potential ... These are the keys that will unlock the door to personal excellence.* ~ **Confucius**

In hindsight, I should have determined my educational journey based on my goals for my life, not on the expectations of others. I should have had higher aspirations than my grandfather had for me. I have learned that only you can determine your climb or your ceiling. Even those who care about you will give you advice informed by their own life experience, fears, and doubts. Do your own due diligence, and let your decisions be driven by your inner pros-and-cons list.

- Data, not anecdotal information, should drive your decision.
- Ask advice from those equipped to give it. I ask my friend who's a great baker for tips on pies; I don't ask her what she thinks about global compensation trends.
- Be a futurist. Create a vision of who you want to become or what you want to achieve.
- Let optimism, not fear, drive your choices.

CHAPTER 8

The First Job

"The most important thing to remember is this: To be ready at any moment to give up what you are for what you might become." ~ **W. E. B. Du Bois**

Chapter Soundtrack: "Respect" ~ Aretha Franklin, 1967

I began working in human resources as a recruiter right out of the gate. This was my first real job after college. This introduction to human resources was a key foundation to my career development. I found recruiting to be fascinating, particularly as a new college graduate who suddenly had the ability to change someone's life with a new job opportunity.

I could hear the desperation from both a candidate and a hiring manager, with each seeking their version of closure. I became adept at reassuring both parties that I would facilitate the best outcome for each of them.

A recruiter is a matchmaker of sorts. A hiring manager details the competencies and attributes they're looking for, and I find the closest match. However, a hiring manager falls in love with the candidate they feel best mirrors them or the company culture. And sometimes they even fall in love with Ivy League credentials. I often had to help a leader select what they need versus a candidate they found witty or interesting but who didn't have the needed skill set.

My background as a recruiter has given me great insight as an interviewee. I love interviewing and am a quick study of the person asking me questions. First of all, I can quickly discern what they're looking for in a candidate. Once you've done so, it's easy to align what you bring to the table with what they need. You also must do your homework, and social media makes that easy. I research information about the company, then find out everything I can about each person I'll meet. Where did they grow up? What college did they attend? Do they have hobbies or awards? It's all valuable to know.

Unfortunately, it was at this first job that I experienced a disturbing racial incident that oddly led to me becoming extraordinarily good friends with a coworker.

I had a boss who treated me differently because of my race—not for any other reason. Both my coworker and I had similar high performance and client-satisfaction ratings, but our manager seemed to magnify any minor mistake I made and constantly critiqued only how I handled client interactions.

When I was faced with this behavior, I didn't want to believe it was racism. But then a White colleague told me, "No! She's definitely treating you differently." After one particularly targeted critique of my work practice, this manager fired me. To my surprise, my friend quit as a result. She said, "There's no way Barbara should have been fired. It's wrong. I quit."

Her allyship led to an executive at the company meeting with both of us to understand what had happened. As a result, the manager was disciplined and my friend and I were both reinstated. I still was wary of that manager, but she now knew her behavior was under scrutiny.

Although the way I was treated hadn't directly impacted her, my friend instinctively understood what she was witnessing and understood her privilege. She understood she was being treated preferentially and that I was being treated poorly simply because of the color of my skin. As a result of that, I got a consequence she never would have received.

She had the rare cultural competency that people talk about now. An awareness of diversity, inclusion, and equity in the workplace wasn't common thirty years ago. There wasn't the broad call to action for anti-racism that we see today. I've had a journey as a woman, as a woman of color, as a woman of color who's a mother, and as a woman of color who's a mother working in a male-dominated environment. All of those layered identities led to all sorts of experiences with bias.

Writing this book is helping me understand a lot of my life lessons from all of these experiences. Black people will say, "I don't trust White people." And White people have these monolithic misconceptions about Black people. My story of a White colleague who made a sacrifice for me when I didn't even think our friendship was worthy of her courageous actions still resonates with me. She epitomized allyship and why it will take all of us to turn the corner to eradicate racism.

Over the years, I've shared this story with others, and people are touched by what she did in my defense. She is still a strong-willed and principled person, and I never forget what she did and the professional and personal risk she took. She had bills to pay and was planning a wedding, yet she lived her values in a way that most do not. I hope this story inspires others to stand up for what they believe to be right in the workplace—even if it comes with negative consequences.

CHAPTER 9

Marriage and Divorce

"Divorce isn't such a tragedy. A tragedy's staying in an unhappy marriage, teaching your children the wrong things about love. Nobody ever died of divorce." ~ **Jennifer Weiner**

Chapter Soundtrack: "What's Love Got to Do with It" ~ recorded by Tina Turner, 1993

I continued to date the college boyfriend, and for years we created a pattern of breaking up and getting back together. I even relocated to Washington, D.C., after graduation to be with him. After one particularly dramatic breakup, I moved out of the apartment we shared and started dating other people. This seemed to impress upon him that he might lose his codependent partner.

He would see me at events or gatherings or hear through mutual friends that I was seeing other people. Apparently, it was a bit of a wake-up call. Several months later he proposed, and suddenly we were engaged.

In hindsight, I'm still not sure why I said yes to his proposal. It was clear that our relationship wasn't a healthy one for me. My first clue was his lack of respect for me and my boundaries. Most therapists, psychologists, and marriage counselors will tell you that the first clue they have in therapy that a marriage won't last is the lack of respect one or both partners have for each other.

Recognizing lack of respect in a personal relationship is a skill that you can use in a professional relationship as well. Examples are not being invited to meetings, included in memos, or offered training that's offered to your peers. Learning to recognize disrespect from friends, family, colleagues, bosses, etc. can tip you off to a need to change, confront a situation, or leave a relationship or job.

It's not unusual that, after so many years dating someone, you begin to believe marriage is the only outcome that equates with success. It would be difficult to live with the fact that you wasted your time in a relationship and feel judgment from friends and family.

My family and friends were thrilled for me when I got engaged. Meanwhile, I was caught up with work, planning the wedding, and trying to see what was possible with our modest budget. My family helped pay for some smaller items, like the cake and a limo, but my future husband and I paid the remainder. Was I happy? Was the relationship healthy and replenishing? No, I wasn't, and it wasn't. But I can't blame him for my inability to establish my boundaries and expectations in our relationship.

I chose what was familiar in a romantic partner: someone who could be critical, controlling, and dismissive of my needs and feelings. My blinders were on. I was seeking the security and structure I'd yearned for in my childhood, and I ignored all the warning signs.

> *I wish I had understood—and that all women would understand—that your relationship with your father is deeply embedded in your subconscious. Fathers have such an incredible impact on their daughters. When we begin to date, it's inevitable that we'll pick partners who have attributes similar to our fathers' attributes. It may be packaged differently, but we subconsciously seek what we grew up with. Without therapy to help us identify what's healthy to expect from a romantic relationship, we won't choose wisely. Our "picker" is off.*
>
> *A woman who grows up with a supportive, loving relationship with her father makes better choices in who she dates, who she sleeps with, and who she marries.*
>
> *To find and participate in a loving, satisfying, committed relationship, you have to deal with your daddy issues. If you don't, you'll select a partner through a distorted filter.*

After we married, we established a pretty normal routine, with both of us working and socializing both together and separately. We worked in telecommunications, and we were doing well in our careers. I was making slightly more than he was, and it stung his ego a bit. We still had disagreements, and I bit my tongue for the sake of the relationship. But I had concerns about how we interacted with each other. I didn't always feel cared for or respected. I told myself to just keep trying, as I didn't want to fail at marriage.

Despite this, we decided to start a family. Yes, I know it makes no sense, but I thought it would make us closer and perhaps make him more settled and more present with his own family. We ultimately had three beautiful children—a girl and then a girl and a boy (twins). As a mother, I found myself experiencing a type of love I hadn't known existed.

Let me be clear about having three children under the age of three: you haven't truly multitasked until you've nursed twins at the same time. I like schedule and routine, and those damn kids didn't get the memo. I remember being half asleep and nursing the twins in the middle of the night. Just as I was in the midst of burping my son, he vomited down my neck and back. I burst into tears, then his sister began crying. And we all just cried for half an hour.

The next day, a friend who worked and had no children called and talked about she'd been shopping for new shoes and had pampered herself over the weekend with a manicure. She finished the story with her travel plans for the month. While she was talking, my two-and-half-year-old threw a stuffed animal at me and knocked the phone out of my hand. It was fate. That call clearly needed to end.

Once all three children were walking, the fun really began: finger painting, trips to the playground and petting zoos, and sandbox play. I was often exhausted by nap time and took a snooze too! I would call the kids my little ducklings, and they would line up in a row behind me on trips to stores. People would laugh and point! Our disciplined procession never lasted long, but I tried.

My then-husband also clearly loved his children and loved being a father. There was always a huge smile on his face when he got home from work, and the kids were always excited to see him. He'd walk in the house and announce, "Daddy's home!" and all the children would be excited. They'd walk, crawl, and squeal while trying to get a hug or a kiss. I would share cute stories about our day, and all of this happy chaos gave me some hope. Meanwhile, our problematic marriage churned along in the background.

I immersed myself in motherhood and believed that our joint love for our children would be enough. I'd stopped working and become a stay-at-home mother, which further shifted the power dynamic in our marriage. I was on a very tight leash. I couldn't make minor decisions without permission. Even decorating the house was full of conflict and rules: no floral, no patterns, no colors beyond what he allowed, etc.

Basically, our roles were suddenly very defined. He came from a family in which his mother and father followed very gender-specific patterns. I was responsible for the well-being of the kids, cooking all meals, keeping the house clean, planning our social life, etc. As the sole breadwinner, his life revolved around work, going to happy hours, golfing, and occasionally "babysitting" his own kids so I could get a break.

My biggest pet peeve is when men are applauded for changing their child's diapers or taking their kids to the park. Yet there I was, living some antiquated 1950s sitcom life, asking my husband for money and permission to leave the house. Women just don't receive recognition or acknowledgement for caregiving.

Having a stay-at-home job is the most exhausting, stressful experience ever. You love your kids and you're grateful for the ability to care for them, but it's hard not to resent your partner. You're alone a lot when you have small children. Even going to the supermarket with three children under three was nearly impossible. You remember what it was like to eat lunch with work colleagues and receive praise for an accomplishment. Now your day involves grape jelly smeared on your arm, along with an assortment of other suspicious substances, and knowing every Raffi song by heart. I hope that I never hear "Baby Beluga" again. I joined a group for mothers of color called Mocha Moms, and it helped to have adult interaction. Those playgroups, moms' nights out, and community service events were lifesavers.

I don't want to appear ungrateful that I had the good fortune of having the time with my children. But I admit that I found it draining, and I worried about losing my identity as anything other than a mother. Options exist now, such as hybrid schedules and the ability to telework, that weren't available to me then. I would have benefited from that flexibility and could have possibly worked part time.

At one point my then-husband took an assignment that meant he was gone Monday through Thursday. That would be impactful to a healthy marriage, much less one that wasn't. I desperately clung to the concept of having a solid family unit, despite the lump in my throat and tearful conversations with my mother. I received advice that "marriage is hard" and that if I sucked it up, it would get better.

A very blunt friend said that being a single parent is hard and that many people stay together for the sake of their kids. While I knew she was right, I was miserable and felt like I was sleepwalking at times. I wondered if I was selfish. I asked myself if I should just tough it out. I decided to seek help because I knew I was showing signs of depression.

I spent many months working with a therapist to rebuild my self-esteem and confront my anxieties and choices. I hadn't worked for several years and was worried about my ability to support myself and the kids if my marriage ended. Moreover, I knew it wouldn't be easy to exit the marriage.

I did little more than cry through the first two sessions. *How could I be in this position?* I wondered. I felt so vulnerable and guilty to be questioning my life and the impact of any decision on my children. Eventually, I made the agonizing decision to separate from my husband. I'm deliberately not going to go into details out of respect for my children but ending a marriage can be a traumatic experience for a family—and it was for us.

> *Did you know that 70% of women file for divorce? Studies also show that there are multiple phases of divorce: grief, denial, anger, bargaining, depression, and lastly, acceptance. Unfortunately, there's no uniform time frame for getting to the final stage of acceptance, and many people stay in denial and anger too long.*[x]

A protracted divorce and custody process can also be very traumatizing to children. If you find yourself dealing with divorce, try your best to be respectful to each other and understand that children shouldn't be weaponized.

CHAPTER 10

Single Motherhood: A Whole Different Ball Game

"One thing I had learned from watching chimpanzees with their infants is that having a child should be fun." ~ **Jane Goodall**

Chapter Soundtrack: "All I Really Need" ~ Raffi, 1979

Being a single mom is not ideal. And juggling three elementary school-aged children is not a walk in the park. There are, however, many perks:

- The toilet seat is always down.
- Shared custody means you get some weekends off.
- You can work out whenever you want.
- You don't have to consult with someone else about any decisions.

- You could make peanut butter and jelly for dinner, and the kids would be thrilled.
- You can't have an argument with yourself.

My kids were my anchors and gave me an enhanced sense of purpose during this time of transition. I knew I needed to be strong and steady to help establish our new normal.

My eldest child had and still has a very intense personality. I definitely saw parallels between her and me in her perfectionism, as well as in her need for control and structure. I felt a great deal of guilt for having added change to her life.

Meanwhile, my twins had more easy-going personalities, but the back and forth of visitation and different rules, bedtimes, and homework expectations caused them a great deal of anxiety and resulted in their acting out. I, too, struggled with anxiety. And like children often do, my kids expressed their anger and frustration to me and at me through temper tantrums. They even told me they hated me for leaving their father.

The love I feel for my children and the love I received from them sustained me even when I doubted my mothering skills. Watching them grow and adapt and learn how to navigate the world fascinated me endlessly—when I allowed myself to breathe and observe. There always seemed to be homework to help with, laundry to keep going, or emails to catch up on because I left work before others. Learning to live in the moment was a struggle.

Their dad, meanwhile, struggled with being a single parent when he had the kids. Visits were often tumultuous, and managing schoolwork, soccer, swim team, birthday parties, and playdates was new to him. He suddenly had to figure out how to do his daughters' hair. He became surprisingly good at it.

I remember talking to an administrator at my children's school and sharing that I felt so bad that my kids had divorced parents. She replied kindly, "Don't worry. Half the class will be made up of divorced families by high school." She was right.

> *There are 11 million single-parent families in the U.S. Single moms make up 8.5 million of those families. Single dads make up the remaining 2.5 million families.*[xi] www.statista.com

I also had to dive back into the workforce. Being a single working mother is a logistical puzzle. How do you get everyone to school, get to work, attend school events, and handle the dreaded "kid wakes up with a fever" dilemma?

I've worked in human resources and operations throughout my career. While working remotely or having a flexible schedule is normalized now (largely due to the pandemic as I write this), it wasn't normal ten to fifteen years ago. I recall taking my sick eight-year-old son with me to work and making him a cozy sleeping bag area under my desk. I had a big meeting that I felt I couldn't miss without a consequence. Several doses of Children's Tylenol and five juice boxes later, his fever broke by five in the evening.

I waited until my boss left for the day, then I quickly gathered all the toys and items I had brought to keep my son occupied. I carried them and him to my car, hoping I didn't catch anyone's attention.

> *"I think every working mom probably feels the same thing: You go through big chunks of time where you're just thinking, 'This is impossible—oh, this is impossible.' And then you just keep going and keep going, and you sort of do the impossible."* ~ **Tina Fey**

Another time I had a boss who, without notice, decided on an early morning meeting the following day. I immediately had to find someone to help my kids get to school because this new meeting time screwed up my finely tuned schedule. Fortunately, a friend offered to help, so I dodged a bullet. Several weeks later my boss again decided to have an early-morning meeting the next day. As the only woman in the room, I mustered up my courage to say, "Mike, I don't have anyone to take care of my kids at seven. I have after-school care, but in the morning it's just me."

Mike looked at me with a frown. "There's no one you can get to watch them?" he asked. Now I was feeling a bit annoyed. "Mike," I said, "who gets your kids ready for school?" He said that his wife did. "Well, I don't have one of those, so I'm simply asking for more notice. Or is it possible to start the meetings at nine, as before?" Thank goodness at that point, some of my male colleagues began to speak up and share that the early meetings were impacting their family schedules as well. It was agreed that we would keep the meeting at nine and give more notice of changes in the future.

After the meeting, one of my coworkers said he was glad I had spoken up. But I worried that I may have harmed myself by doing so. I had to be extra careful not to be labeled as an "angry Black woman" or a bitch. Being assertive can be a double-edged sword.

The problem is that you're never quite sure when the stereotypes will be applied to you. That's why it's so important to build allyship or specifically ask for it from your colleagues—particularly your male colleagues. The topic of allyship is being spoken of more frequently, so I hope that more people will speak up or stand up for others without having to be asked.

Interestingly enough, I have often had great male colleagues. Some have been mentors, and others have been peers or simply buddies. Hearing different perspectives about a work dilemma or just seeing how direct and aggressive male colleagues could be with other men helped me build workplace insight. Sometimes male coworkers had inside-track information that all the men were discussing when I wasn't around. Lastly, my male colleagues would invite me to meetings or events and tacitly vouch for me.

> *There's a pervasive pressure in the workplace that I find is particularly placed on women: you must almost act as if you have no children or responsibilities that may distract you from your work duties. We have to be a superwoman, balancing the need to be a great mother with our desire to excel in our career. It's truly unfair and often impossible.*
>
> *I wish I'd felt as empowered in the past as I do now to speak up when decisions disproportionately impact women. I had not truly embraced, as I do now, the full scope of my personal power and how to influence outcomes.*

As a single mother, I felt stretched thin. I was ambitious and deeply focused on moving up the leadership ranks. First, I knew I was capable and was making up for time I'd lost as a stay-at-home mom. And second, I wanted to provide a financially stable reality for my children.

> *"Children are not a distraction from more important work, they are the most important work."* ~ **C. S. Lewis**

I made a lot of mistakes, though. I was often stressed and was not the best version of myself or as patient as I could have been with my children. I can't tell you how many times I was late for work because someone announced they'd forgotten a homework assignment or musical instrument just as we were almost to school.

Still, I would turn around, get the missed item, go back to school to drop it off, then anxiously race to work. There were also wonderful times when we would all be snuggled on the couch watching a movie, with the kids lying half on top of me. At those times, I could exhale and just enjoy the moment.

Eventually my finances were stable enough that the kids could attend aftercare at school, and I could hire a babysitter to pick them up and take them home or to a practice. Then I could come home, make dinner, have some breathing room, and enjoy spending time with them instead of rushing around.

One of my biggest regrets is that I initially didn't know how to carve out time for self-care. I felt guilty going to the gym or doing anything other than kid-related activities. I had primary care of the kids, so they were with me the majority of the time. I didn't set boundaries or leverage my extended family initially, and certainly dating felt impossible.

> *It's so important for single mothers to do replenishing things to recharge their batteries, whether it's time to read a book or go to the gym or plant flowers in the yard. You deserve time to pursue these activities. Without any other interests or time to replenish, your resilience to stress and life's daily challenges just drops to an unsustainable level. Your children need to see you as a person with needs, not as a robot built to serve everyone's needs but her own.*

Eventually, my mother and my aunts often came and stayed with the kids during the summer months to help me out. The kids looked forward to this. To my delight, they loved these visits with family. My mother was particularly happy, and she was very indulgent with them. I would come home to wonderful meals and desserts. My oldest would tease me and say, "I love Grandma more than you." Hell, I was in love with grandma visits too. There was no debate on my part.

Looking back on my life, my challenges, my successes, my failures, and how I overcame or pivoted throughout high school, college, and my first job, I realized the one thing women, including myself, most often fail to learn: their value. And by value, I mean who they are as a person and the value they have to offer others in relationships, friendships, marriage, and jobs.

While social currency—"if you do this, I'll do that"—and how we negotiate our value as friends, spouses, and colleagues is one thing, knowing your financial worth is another topic altogether. While there are dozens of life lessons I can share from my past, the most important one is how to negotiate and know your worth. It's so important that I'm devoting an entire chapter to it. Enjoy. And then put it to work. You're worth more than you know.

CHAPTER 11

How to Negotiate: Knowing Your Worth

"The most common way people give up their power is by thinking they don't have any." ~ **Alice Walker**

Chapter Soundtrack: "She Works Hard for the Money" ~ Donna Summer, 1983

Money is something I'm very comfortable discussing—perhaps because I spent a great deal of my life seeking financial stability. However, many people—especially women—aren't comfortable with money or talking about it. They struggle to state very clearly what their financial value is to their organization. I think this comes from societal norms placed upon women to be modest and nonconfrontational, or from just wanting to be liked.

I have counseled hundreds of people on how to ask for a raise or negotiate a job offer. Now, let's be pragmatic: you have to be good at what you do, have a skill that's in strong demand, or be very knowledgeable about something critical. And a company must see your value if you're going to ask for more money. In addition, it's helpful to have allies or mentors in your organization who have influence and can support a promotion or raise for you.

Do your homework. Work to understand your value in the marketplace. Have you queried your network? Do you belong to professional organizations that do salary surveys? Are you on headhunters' radar screens? Is your social media updated to highlight your accomplishments? You owe it to yourself to know and be able to articulate how you add value to your company.

Some important tips:

- Determine what you want. Is it a 15% salary increase or a title change?
- Understand that this is all about negotiation, preparedness, and leverage.
    - Know your company's policies on promotions and salary adjustments.
    - Know who has been promoted in the past year; understand or ask about their process.
- Role-play your discussion with a trusted colleague or family member.
    - You need to be able to speak concisely about your accomplishments and demonstrate value and impact.

- DO schedule time to speak with your boss, in person or by video conference.
- DO NOT use email to convey your request.
- When you meet, be bright, be brief, and be gone—especially if you get a yes.
- If you get a no, ask for the reason. It's okay to respectfully express disappointment. I always suggest asking when the conversation can be revisited or what's needed for a promotion, salary increase, etc.
    - Analyze the reasons given. Are they reasonable? Are you getting a clear message that you're not viewed as critical to the company?
    - Regroup and don't get bogged down with negative thoughts.

It's important to be comfortable with negotiation and conflict. Sometimes these conversations aren't easy. You need to own your personal power and make sure your boss understands that whatever you're asking for needs to be strongly considered. Unfortunately, if your discussions are disappointing, you may need to assess your value outside your organization and find a company that does see your potential. Just because you were told no doesn't mean the issue is you and your skills. Some companies may not have the budget. I certainly have had this experience, as have most people at one time or another. This should not be earth shattering—people will have many professional opportunities in their lifetimes.

The average number of jobs in a lifetime is twelve, according to a 2019 Bureau of Labor Statistics (BLS) survey of baby boomers.

Workers had an average of 4.5 jobs when they were twenty-five to thirty-four years old, and 2.9 jobs when they were thirty-five to forty-four years old. During the most established phase of many workers' careers, ages forty-five to fifty-two, they held only an average of 1.9 jobs.[xii]

Ultimately, some of us will change jobs for career progression, and some will have lengthy tenures at one organization. The key is to be confident that your contributions are recognized and that you're competitively compensated. Finding a company that checks all the boxes can be like dating you'll kiss a lot of frogs.

PART 3

The Messy Middle - I Think I'm Getting the Hang of This

CHAPTER 12

The Professional Arc

"Life will give you whatever experience is most helpful for the evolution of your consciousness." ~ **Eckhart Tolle**

Chapter Soundtrack: "You Gotta Be" ~ Des'ree, 1994

People are fascinating packages of contradictions, inspiration, sacrifice, loyalty, hope, and so much more. That's why I love interacting with people. I'm eternally curious about them and what makes them tick. I want to understand each one and how they came to be the person they are.

I want to know if we've shared similar experiences and how they dealt with victories, trauma, and pain. Was their path similar to mine, or not? There's no judgment there. Just curiosity.

In other words, I naturally care to discover what matters to those I meet. To me there's nothing more exciting than walking into a room full of strangers. It's like a light switch turns on in my heart. I know for sure there's a certain possibility of making a valuable business connection, a potential friend, or even an ally. Even if I don't enjoy a person's company, that's also valuable information to file away.

I want to know people's fears, ambitions, and triggers. I'll ask them to tell me what they like to eat and even stories about their travels. It's a survival tactic I honed in childhood. Who knew that all of those experiences of meeting so many different people through the years would turn into such an asset? If I understand every facet of my environment and the people who inhabit that space, then I have the advantage of insight, leverage, and influence.

My husband and friends are amazed at the intimate details people will share with me so readily. A fellow coach has speculated that it's because I have a deep level of empathy and compassion. I know of life's challenges and want to offer others a safe place where they can be vulnerable, messy, and imperfect.

I've learned that I gain more from helping others achieve rather than exploiting and manipulating what I know about them. I've walked on the dark side and leveraged my knowledge in a way that may have allowed a business objective to be reached, but not in a way that felt authentic to me. Those were times when I emulated colleagues who were labeled successful even if they left a scorched path.

In human resources, you're often positioned to oversee very difficult organizational change. Earlier in my career I lacked the confidence, influence, and expertise to push back on organizational decisions that were not employee centric and that I knew would not lead to long-term success. As a woman, I often had my suggestions co-opted or mansplained away. So over time I have learned how and when to stand my ground. My personal brand has evolved to be that of a truth teller and a person who will lean into conflict while striving to seek a mutually agreeable solution.

If you find yourself at a point of conflict, I suggest that you not make it a win-or-lose exercise. I've had many conversations that I initially feared to have, all while having to be authentic and aligned with my personal principles. Process your feelings into a narrative that conveys the importance of the topic and what can be gained with a different action or approach. Practice in front of the mirror if you have to or script yourself with notes if that's helpful. But be true to yourself.

Being able to not only survive but thrive in corporate America has been a journey of adaptability, professional growth, and, yes, some failures. I believe my childhood gave me a type of fearlessness. When given an assignment, I simply believe I can accomplish it or meet all expectations. Even if the tremors of anxiety are hovering in the background, I narrow my focus on achieving the goal.

If I encounter an obstacle, I can't sleep until I've determined what the alternative strategy must be. If I fail, I'll pause momentarily and take stock. But it won't stop me from boldly trying again, and it will inform or modify my approach.

This fearlessness has also allowed me to weather subtle and even direct sexism and racism in the workplace. A sometimes-daily battle with microaggressions and biased assumptions has often been my reality. My confidence or assertiveness often met a negative response when my male counterparts were rewarded. Not sure what a microaggression is?

- **"I don't see color. I'm color-blind."**
    - Stating that you're color-blind diminishes or denies the experiences of people of color. Moreover, society <u>does</u> see color and race. It's a privilege to not have to worry about racism and your ethnicity. Acknowledging and appreciating diversity or someone's race doesn't mean you're racist.
- **"Where are you from?" "I'm from Cleveland." "No, I mean where are you and your family originally from?"**
    - Assuming that someone who looks different from you must not be from this country is grounded in bias.
- **Calling a woman "sweetie" or "darling" or touching her body without permission and invading personal space.**

- **Making assumptions and underestimating abilities.**
    - "You have children, so you probably can't work late" or assuming that a person of color isn't the leader in a meeting.

I haven't always fully understood the multitude of ways to lead or use my innate tool kit. For example, as an operational leader, you often influence who gets resources or focus. The keys to being successful are how you make these decisions, how you think about the collective, and whether you take the time to envision the impact it may have on your organization and its people.

I'm decisive but not impulsive. In most cases, I'm a data-driven person and, while it may sound contradictory, I know when emotional intelligence (EQ) trumps reliance on facts and figures. EQ means understanding when to ask, when to push into conflict, when to be quiet and, lastly, when to leave when you get a yes. It also means knowing how to engage with others in a way that's respectful and thoughtful.

> *"You don't make any progress by standing on the sidelines, whimpering and complaining. You make progress by implementing ideas."* ~ **Shirley Chisholm**

However, I do believe that my greatest asset is my ability to connect with other people. If I can unlock potential in staff who report to me, colleagues know I have a vested interest in their success, or I become a trusted thought partner to a CEO, I gain personal fulfillment and they gain a loyal and supportive partner or mentor.

This is what led me to become an executive coach in addition to my daily role as a human resources and operations executive. I believe that coaching is a type of focused mentoring and purposeful guidance that leads to a better understanding of strengths and insights on positive and negative patterns of behavior.

Several years ago, I conducted a coaching session with an extraordinarily gifted woman who was an executive at a large company. She was forty years old and suffered from imposter syndrome. She was a closet introvert, as many women who face these feelings can be.

She'd come from a startup, where she brilliantly handled everything, she had responsibility for, then made a killing in a subsequent merger. During our session, she told me that when she walked into a meeting at her present job, she was often overwhelmed by feelings of inadequacy.

I shared with her that at any point in anyone's life, there are moments when they aren't sure if they can be their authentic self or are worried about what people are thinking of them. We tell ourselves these stories and create narratives, such as, "I really don't belong here. People are probably thinking what I'm saying doesn't make sense or isn't relevant. How did I get this role in the company?"

She replied, "That's exactly what I was thinking in a recent meeting. How did you know I was feeling that way?" I told her that I'd had the same experiences.

It's important for everyone to be mindful that people in any meeting are likely struggling with their own demons. You're not alone in your insecurity or worries about your professional persona. While this is but one issue women can face as they climb the corporate ladder, women of any age may find themselves dealing with similar scenarios. But women just out of high school, in college, or beginning their professional careers can be particularly easily hit with this type of self-doubt.

> *Imposter syndrome can come from being in a certain age demographic or ethnic group, dealing with a disability, or having received a promotion. There are so many reasons why one can have a sense of uncertainty.*

Taking time to look at root causes to better understand how your past experiences, both positive and negative, impact your adult self can be helpful. Having an executive coach can help you build the self-awareness you need to overcome what's holding you back from professional satisfaction or success.

It used to be very common for employees who were struggling professionally to be directed to coaching. Now coaching is actually sought out by new CEOs or entire leadership teams that are seeking new ways to address challenges or accelerate team synergy. Investing in yourself is never a bad idea. In fact, it often makes the difference in overcoming professional or life challenges. And by investing, I mean professional training, therapy, life coaching, or academic pursuits. Investing means being willing to put in the time, money, effort, and work to improve who you are and where you're going.

Coaching has also allowed me to pay it forward. All the mentors and bosses who put faith in me and encouraged me are manifested in how I seek to positively impact the lives of others. This has karmic implications. Some say that everything you do creates either a positive or negative consequence.

> The Oxford dictionary defines karma as:
>
> Noun (in Hinduism and Buddhism) the sum of a person's actions in this and previous states of existence, viewed as deciding their fate in future existences.
>
> - INFORMAL
>   destiny or fate, following as effect from cause.[XIII]

In essence, I believe that coaching or mentoring has allowed me to personally flourish. This cyclical concept of having an awareness of how your actions can put in motion larger causes and effects is one that most people can adopt. Think about your last important business decision. Did it feel authentic? Did your team or peers feel they fully understood your motivation? Heck, do you understand your motivation? Were you scared to make a mistake? Were you simply emulating what others have done?

Coaching can connect you to your deepest strengths and allow you to see your true self. It can help you push through fear of failure or the stresses of each day by helping you create coping mechanisms or strategies. It can help you find internal balance so that the true version of yourself—that confident voice in your head—is amplified. It's like you just found that brightness scale on your iPhone, and photos and messages are now easier to see.

> "You don't become what you want, you become what you believe." ~ **Oprah Winfrey**

CHAPTER 13

Role Model: Burden or Gift?

"If I've impacted on one heart, one mind, one soul, and brought to that individual a greater truth than that individual came into a relationship with me having, then I would say that I have been successful." ~ **Harry Belafonte**

Chapter Soundtrack: "Survivor" ~ Destiny's Child, 2002

I have often been the only woman or the only person of color on the senior team in many of the organizations I've worked in. It's challenging to be the only one who sees the world through a different lens. Moreover, you're encouraged or even pressured to cloak or diminish those differences to succeed.

You're continually and overtly reminded that you're fitting into a specific culture and must adapt versus asking the culture to change for you. It's at this point where I look back and am grateful for my childhood and college experiences. I couldn't always see it at the time, but I know now that those seemingly small (and large) challenges were preparing me for who I am today.

Not being part of the dominant culture taught me that I have to work harder to build relationships when those relationships don't come looking for me. I'm not asked to play golf because people assume I don't play. I wasn't automatically invited to drinks after work. My otherness was demonstrated to me time and time again—something my childhood exposed me to and prepared me for.

My work had to be outstanding. It was scrutinized, and mistakes or errors were sometimes used almost like evidence to show that I wasn't worthy. Outstanding successes were labeled as luck rather than indicators of business prowess and my hard work.

> *"The only thing that separates women of color from everyone else is opportunity."* ~ **Viola Davis**

There was no ability to complain. I would only damage myself by pointing out bias or exclusion. My strategy was to build strong teams that were proactive, talented, and universally respected by other leaders. I volunteered for the conflict-laden projects that my colleagues didn't want. I noted birthdays, work anniversaries, and special events. I even attended funerals to ensure my presence was seen and my colleagues knew that I cared. The culmination of these efforts was greater acceptance, and by my efforts I made myself indispensable.

It is another full-time job to be the exceptional minority. Other women and employees of color would seek my help, guidance, and mentorship. I can't count how many cups of coffee I consumed meeting with staff who felt their careers weren't progressing, or women asking how to juggle childcare or deal with the guilt of leaving a newborn at home. These coffee dates and discussions informed my advocacy for my organizations to create policies and practices that were employee friendly or just equitable.

This advocacy extended to providing opinions on promotions and high-profile projects to staff members. There was all sorts of bias, assumptions, and ageism, such as, "This employee is too young to take on this assignment" or "This female employee has young children, so she probably can't travel." Then there is the Black employee who some feel is not the right fit, but no one can explain why.

I can recall many occasions when I had to take a deep breath, center myself, and professionally challenge colleagues on their assumptions. I always wonder what would happen if I hadn't been in the room. I have had to decide when and how to be a truth teller in a meeting or a one-on-one conversation. It's a skill that didn't come easily and was founded on my upbringing, as well as a lifetime of learning people skills and developing my emotional intelligence.

What are *unconscious biases*?

Unconscious biases, also known as implicit biases, are the underlying attitudes and stereotypes that people unconsciously attribute to another person or group of people that affect how they understand and engage with a person or group. This can lead to unsupported conclusions in favor of or against one person or group as compared to another.

How does *unconscious bias* happen?

Unconscious bias is a result of our limited cognitive capacity. The brain's automatic, unconscious sifting and sorting of visual, verbal, and behavioral cues means that we develop unintentional people preferences. Attitudes and stereotypes form that affect our actions and decisions in an unconscious way and can cause us to make incorrect deductions based on flawed logic or data.[xiv]

I've decided that being a role model is both a gift and a burden. It would be easier to adopt the mindset that I'm responsible for myself only. But I'm unable to do that. If my voice can make a difference, then I have an obligation to leverage my influence—regardless of professional risk. Let's be clear: there are those who don't want to be reminded that there are no women or BIPOC being interviewed for a key role. My voice and opinions aren't always welcomed or appreciated. That doesn't mean I don't voice them. In a world where silence is perceived more as approval or agreement, it's important to speak up even if your point of view isn't appreciated. It's heard, and that matters.

This may be an oversimplification, but as a parent, I want the world to evolve and change for my children and for everyone's children. The rolling back of voter rights, the existence of racism, and having children who will face the same challenges I experienced is disheartening. However, anyone reading this book can help move forward the change that's needed to ensure our workplaces, our country, and our world is free of bias and equitable for all.

Three things to think about:

- Speak up if you see or perceive that unconscious bias is driving a business decision.
- See the humanity of Black people, I should not have to be exceptional at sports, business, or music to matter.
- Please, please act like you have a vested interest in the success of others.
- Every man who sees a woman being treated inappropriately should remember that she could be his mother, his sister, his niece, or his daughter.

CHAPTER 14

How to Talk About Diversity, Equity, and Inclusion (DEI)

"Our ability to reach unity in diversity will be the beauty and the test of our civilization." ~ **Mahatma Gandhi**

Chapter Soundtrack: "Move on Up" ~ Curtis Mayfield, 1970

It's a new day, and the ability to have conversations about diversity, equity, and inclusion is not only necessary, but critically important, professionally, and personally. Social pressures for fair and equitable business practices and environments have been building over the last few decades. Pay equity, diversity, antiracism, and antiharassment have emerged as critical issues. Further urgency was created by the tragedy of George Floyd's death, and the

Time's Up and #MeToo movements spotlighting sexual harassment.

Diversity is all around us. It can be identified as race and ethnicity, gender and gender identity, sexual orientation, socioeconomic status, language, culture, national origin, religious beliefs and identity, age, disability status, and political perspective. Your confidence in navigating our complex world can be how you differentiate yourself as a leader and a human being.

It can be scary to wade into a conversation about diversity and how we're the same or different. You may find that some aspects of a person's diverse characteristics may not be visible, and you may make a mistake or a microaggression (more on that later). To magnify the degree of difficulty, we're living in such polarizing times that everything has become politicized and respectful discourse isn't the norm. But wade in you must.

Some tips on how to engage:

- Respect everyone's identity and don't make assumptions or create a story about anyone without getting to know them. It's too easy to fall into stereotyping people of any color or background.
- You CAN ask questions to determine an individual's preferences about their identity or pronouns. Most people won't be offended if you make it clear that there's no ill intent, just a desire to understand and be respectful.

    - An example might be asking a coworker if you should use *Black* or *African American* or asking another colleague on preferences on the use of *Latina* or *Hispanic* as a descriptor.
    - Gender identity is about how people sees themselves. Sexual orientation is who one may be attracted to. Learn the appropriate terminology: *bi*, *cis*, *gay*, *lesbian*, etc.
- Don't use outdated or offensive stereotypical language or labels.
    - A person who is blind is not disabled. They have a disability.

When I engage in dialogue on this topic, I've become quite agile at meeting people where they are. I'm a businesswoman, a wife, a parent, a sister, and, yes, a person of color. I can find some commonality, shared experience, skill, or preference, and that's where I find connection. I find that opening, then I step right in there to see and be seen.

There's one thing I know to be true, and that's that chaos, anger, and dysfunction don't result in a good or sustainable outcome. Do you want to run a business where employees are extraordinarily productive and loyal to you? What about a satisfied, diverse client or patron base? Do you want to create an inclusive brand or one that limits your outreach?

We want to sell products to anyone who wants to buy them. We want to perform music for anyone who will pay to listen. We want tourists to come to our country and have a positive experience and enhance our economy. Bias regarding someone's sexual orientation, gender, or race is simply flawed logic to me.

Look at the global landscape. America's competitive advantage is its diversity. No other country can recruit from such a diverse talent pool or take advantage of the wealth of experience that talent pool brings. There's also a false narrative that cultural competence is some type of overcorrection. That somehow the pendulum has swung too far left.

I need to fact-check some things. There was a time in the not too distant past when it was legal to enslave a Black person. It was also legal to segregate people and deny them the right to vote. The legacy of this and so much more ties us to a past that must be acknowledged, learned from, and renounced.

> *"I have come to believe over and over again that what is most important to me must be spoken, made verbal and shared, even at the risk of having it bruised or misunderstood."* – **Audre Lorde**

I have facilitated hundreds of training sessions on DEI. Even disinterested audiences can experience enlightenment or have stereotypical beliefs reversed for them. I don't think training is the cure to change long-held biases, but it may be a catalyst to get people discussing the issues that both align and separate them.

The world is getting smaller and smaller, and its eco-system and resources are becoming more fragile. The violence shown toward one another is transparently evil and undeniable. We must be better. There simply is no other choice. It's both an individual and collective choice to turn toward goodness and compassion. I know what choice I'm making. Do you?

> *"Let's stop believing that our differences make us superior or inferior to one another."* ~ **Don Miguel Ruiz**

CHAPTER 15

Facing Your Fears

"The brave man is not he who does not feel afraid, but he who conquers that fear." ~ **Nelson Mandela**

Chapter Soundtrack: "Smile" ~ Kirk Franklin, 2011

Everyone has fears and anxiety, some rational and some irrational. I've learned that you must get to the core of the fears, particularly those that are blocking you from achieving a goal. How you get there is your choice but getting to a place where you can walk through your fears is critical.

Some options that can be helpful:

- **Therapy** – I've found therapy to be a very healthy way to understand how my past may be blocking my future endeavors.
- **A mentor or coach** – Look for someone who can provide a safe place to deconstruct your "why."

- **Meditation** – This is a way to quiet all the noise around you and clear your mind to make sound decisions.
- **Mindfulness** – Press pause on your typical responses, perspectives, and even your words, then think about how you might reframe to serve yourself and others better.
- **Exercise** – Try kickboxing. Punching the hell out of something and releasing negative energy can help you gain clarity.
- **Disrupting your life and prioritizing yourself** – I've taken a break from my life and gone on vacation. This doesn't have to be expensive. Sometimes just spending a long weekend with a friend or family member gives you enough distance from your normal life. I once spent a week in New Mexico at a relaxing retreat just for me and returned rejuvenated with renewed energy for the issues I needed to deal with.
- **Reflection** – What lessons can you learn from your experiences? How did you cope with challenges in your childhood, college, career, or parenting? What would you do differently? What did you learn?

What would happen if you did the thing, you fear most? Here's the thing: You don't know. So why are you predicting a negative outcome? This is why a lot of our fears are absolutely illogical. I believe many of our fears thrive in the dark parts of our minds where we don't want to experience failure or loss. But we're more resilient than we think. Often, even the failure we experience is modest in comparison to what we feared it would be.

Alternatively, if the failure you experience is as bad as you imagined, can you not rebound or seek help from those who care for you?

> *"Even though you may want to move forward in your life, you may have one foot on the brakes. In order to be free, we must learn how to let go. Release the hurt. Release the fear. Refuse to entertain your old pain. The energy it takes to hang onto the past is holding you back from a new life. What is it you would let go of today?"*
> ~ **Mary Manin Morrissey**

Am I an optimist? Yes, I am. And I'm pretty sure I have a higher number of good days than bad because of it. It may seem too crunchy granola, but life has the potential to throw everything at you separately or even all at once. I want to cling hard to the potential of happiness rather than the certainty of misfortune.

This perspective, by the way, can be oddly radical to some. When I tell someone that I choose to believe in the possibility of a positive outcome, it doesn't mean I'm not prepared for a less-than-desirable reality. However, think deeply on this: if I spend more time preparing for a negative outcome versus a positive one, how is this the best use of my time? It's unfortunate that it's easier to believe the bad than the good, but it doesn't mean that you should.

My message is clear: you can choose how you want to experience life. My grandparents and great-grandparents experienced things that should have left them bitter and jaded. Instead, their legacy was one of joy, family, and sacrifice for others. Look for those examples around you or behind you, and let that inform how you address your fear.

> *"People think about the word 'fearless' to mean without fear. I see it to actually mean 'with fear but you do it anyway."* ~ **Luvvie Ajayi Jones**

CHAPTER 16

Wheel of Fortune

> *"You can waste your lives drawing lines. Or you can live your life crossing them."* ~ **Shonda Rhimes**

Chapter Soundtrack: "Beautiful Day"
~ U2, 2000

A follow-up to facing your fears is the mindset to take advantage of opportunities or situations that can help you professionally and personally. Stop saying no to things that seem beyond your abilities or inconvenient to your schedule, or that you worry you might potentially fail at completing.

> *"Men are confident about their ability at 60%, but women don't feel confident until they've checked off each item on the list." The advice: women need to have more faith in themselves."*[xv]

I actually think that, for women, the issue is that they are rule followers. It's less about confidence than it is about them not applying if the job describes a specific skill set that they don't possess. Whether it's finding a job or getting promoted, it's the preparation that's important. It's not a game show like *Wheel of Fortune*.

There are specific strategies and actions you can take for professional growth:

Set professional goals for yourself and aim high. I wanted to serve on a corporate board, so I researched, networked, and identified where I might have the best chance to be considered and selected. Please understand that I mean you should go all the way back to high school (which I did) and seek allies, be proud, and share your accomplishments and talents.

You must tell people what you want to pursue professionally. If you can't specifically identify the opportunities, industries, or companies that are of interest to you, then do your research. Leverage your social media and network with those who may be able to share perspectives and insights to help you on your journey. Seek out those who can introduce you to a decision-maker or a person with influence.

I don't discount the growing number of organizations that exist with the goal of increasing the number of women on boards. I certainly have participated in those efforts and will continue to do so. However, most board opportunities aren't filled by headhunters; they're filled by individuals known by the board or senior executives within the company.

Are you building your brand so you can either attract attention or build your network so that you are thought of when opportunities arise? Women are often not spending hours on the golf course. We're often too heads down and don't even grasp the conversations we're missing. Women aren't mentored and selected as high performers as frequently as men.

The numbers don't lie:

> In May, 2021 Equilar's new Gender Diversity Index *revealed that as of the fourth quarter of 2020, 23.5% of all board seats on the Russell 3000 Index, which tracks the performance of the 3,000 largest public U.S. companies, are held by women. That's an increase from 21.5% in the previous year's fourth quarter, up from 18.5% at the end of 2018, and from 15% at the end of 2016.*
>
> *But while the percentage continues to inch up, 6% of those Russell 3000 Index boards contain no women at all.*
>
> *Bottom line? The pandemic actually has exacerbated the global gender gap, and the World Economic Forum now predicts parity will not be achieved for another 135.6 years, which is up from about 100 years before the crisis hit.*[XVI]

So extraordinary effort will likely be necessary. I can't sugarcoat it. I'm insulted when people say I'm lucky. I'm not lucky. I'm simply focused on what I want to accomplish.

I'm aware of my strengths. I amplify those areas and I don't waste time on tasks that I will, at best, perform at a mediocre level.

It doesn't mean you shouldn't challenge yourself and try to learn new skills. You should, however, assess quickly if practice or exposure to this new area of interest will result in outstanding results or personal satisfaction. If not, you may be wasting energy and brain cells. Value your time better.

Some of us are going to have to work harder and, yes, it's not fair. But it's the truth. I recently told one of my children that while I can empathize when they share that they were treated unfairly, my next question is, What will you do to overcome the obstacle? How can you make the circumstance work in your favor? Fill your resilience bucket. You're going to need it on your journey. Life is likely going to encompass amazing experiences and opportunities and a healthy dose of side-eye.

Spin that wheel and see what options may be in store for you. I'll lend you money to buy a vowel.

PART 4

Adaptability and Resilience – Dust Yourself off and Keep It Moving

CHAPTER 17

When Your Body Lets You Down

"It's not the load that breaks you down, it's the way you carry it." ~ **Lena Horne**

Chapter Soundtrack: "Rise Up" ~ Andra Day, 2015

Right after my fortieth birthday, I began to feel run down. I attributed it to work, motherhood, stress, etc. But after taking my children to the county fair on a sunny summer day, I developed a rash over my cheeks and nose. I thought it was odd. I thought it was maybe just an allergic reaction to something I ate, and it went away after a week. Several months later, I began to have severe joint pain. It was difficult to walk. My feet hurt and I had small but painful bumps on my heels.

I went to my regular doctor, who had no idea what was wrong. He prescribed an antibiotic and painkillers. I struggled for several weeks before deciding to see a specialist. I scheduled an appointment with a rheumatologist because I thought perhaps the joint pain was related to arthritis. The rheumatologist ran lots of tests and took lots of blood. Then he told me he believed I had systemic lupus erythematosus.

> *Systemic lupus erythematosus (SLE), is the most common type of lupus. SLE is an autoimmune disease in which the immune system attacks its own tissues, causing widespread inflammation and tissue damage in the affected organs.*[xvii]

This rheumatologist put me on a massive dosage of prednisone (steroids) and, while my pain and inflammation subsided, I developed a moon face and felt foggy from the drugs. I also put on weight and felt fatigued. After several months of this treatment, I decided to see another rheumatologist who'd been recommended to me, and I'm so glad I did.

This doctor actually listened closely to my issues, the symptoms, and the changes that the steroids were making to my body. She prescribed a different regimen of medications, and we began the slow journey of weaning me down to a minimal steroid dosage. After a year, I began to stabilize and feel more like my pre-lupus diagnosis self. I told very few people—only family initially—because I worried it would impact my trajectory at work if my employer knew I had a chronic medical condition.

Although I was managing my condition fairly successfully, at times I would overdo it and my body let me know it. One day I arrived at work to go on a business trip. I felt fatigued, and my chest and shoulders felt achy. I felt like I was moving in slow motion. Soon the pain in my chest increased. I knew something was very wrong, so I asked my assistant to take me to the hospital.

I was having a lupus flare and clearly needed to take stock of how I was treating my body and balancing my time. This was a wake-up call for me. I couldn't act as if I were this indestructible ball of activity that I had been in the past. I began to be more selective about my time and say no to commitments. When individuals who suffer from lupus have access to good medical care and the appropriate medications as I do, they can have a normal life span.

Lupus Facts:

- The Lupus Foundation of America estimates that **1.5 million** Americans, and at least 5 million people worldwide, have a form of lupus.
- There are many challenges to reaching a lupus diagnosis. Lupus is known as "the great imitator" because its symptoms mimic many other illnesses. Lupus symptoms can also be unclear, can come and go, and can change.

- On average, it takes nearly six years for people with lupus to be diagnosed after they first notice their lupus symptoms.
- Lupus strikes mostly women of child-bearing age. However, men, children, and teenagers develop lupus too.
- Ninety percent of people living with lupus are women. Most people with lupus develop the disease between the ages of fifteen and forty-four.
- Lupus is two to three times more prevalent among women of color—African Americans, Hispanics/Latinos, Asians, Native Americans, Alaska Natives, Native Hawaiians and other Pacific Islanders—than among White women. Recent research indicates that lupus affects 1 in 537 young African American women.[xviii]

I also decided to be more proactive about this disease. I reached out to the Lupus Foundation of America and the Washington, D.C., chapter to see how I could become more involved. I later was invited to join the national board, and, through board service, I have tried to make a difference. Nonprofit board service is a great way to learn how boards operate. You'll certainly be expected to participate in fundraising and as an ambassador, but you'll gain governance insight and new relationships.

Participation on this board has allowed me to gain deeper knowledge about this terrible disease. It also provides me the ability to elevate attention to the disparate health care outcomes that impact those who suffer from it. This advocacy is close to home; resources to eradicate this disease and others should be a focus for our government leaders.

As I'm writing this, the world is still reeling from the aftermath of the COVID-19 pandemic of 2020/2021. I feel like there's a rawness to people now—just such a state of not knowing how things are going to pan out. Life feels more precious. And it should. I now see the need to be a little more vulnerable than I might have been comfortable being ten years ago.

At first I wasn't going to write about this chronic medical condition I live with. My brain's rationale was, "Well, it might harm me professionally if people broadly know." My husband replied, "Look at what you've accomplished despite this health obstacle." As usual, his opinion made perfect sense and brought things into perspective.

Most of us share certain things with just a few people. It often feels like we have to be cautious in revealing our personal struggles. But I've also learned that people want to know that you're vulnerable, and it's okay to show that there are times when you feel REALLY vulnerable. Everyone goes through this, whether it's themselves or a family member.

You still have to work, you still have to get up in the morning, your kids still need you. You still have to deal with people who are less than sympathetic to your issue, and that can be tough. My husband was right. Put it into perspective. Stop and ask yourself, Will this matter in five years? Or ten? Or even two? Put it into perspective and let go of the fear.

The global pandemic has made us all feel exposed, and perhaps we value life differently. I now believe it's important for us to feel free to share more of ourselves, to not be afraid to be transparent. If I can help one person feel like a lupus diagnosis doesn't mean they can't live a full life, then my honesty will be worth it.

"You are your best thing." ~ **Toni Morrison**

CHAPTER 18

Bucket List

"Do not fear mistakes. There are none."
~ **Miles Davis**

Chapter Soundtrack: "Unwritten" ~ Natasha Bedingfield, 2004

I like to challenge myself, take risks, and have fun. And I've learned that carving out time to do this is critically important. I've made lists of things that I want to do and am slowly but surely checking off each item. Let's be clear: some of my selected adventures have been abject failures, but I have no regrets. I hope I can inspire others to create their own bucket list. Trust me on this: you owe it to yourself. Here are some items from my list that might inspire you:

- Do stand-up comedy
- Bungee jump
- Create my own art
- Get a tattoo
- Dye my hair blonde

- Become a certified executive coach
- Try rock climbing
- Place wreaths on soldiers' graves at Arlington National Cemetery
- Visit The National Memorial for Peace and Justice and The Legacy Museum
- Volunteer to feed the hungry
- Dive with sharks
- Take cooking classes
- Drive an ATV in the desert
- Learn how to meditate
- Write a book
- Go on a Hawaiian Islands exploration
- Take a yacht cruise along the Bosphorus

Bucket list item #1: Do stand-up comedy. The good news is that most cities have comedy venues. To make extra money, they offer all sorts of classes, such as: improv, stand-up, and sketch comedy classes. I took the leap and signed up for a four-week class that would culminate with a short stand-up performance. When I arrived at the first class, it hit me. I thought, *Wait a minute. What the heck have I done? Comedy shows have live hecklers, and what if I bomb?*

Fortunately, my fellow aspiring comedians were pretty nice, and most were all equally terrified by what they had signed up to learn. The best part about stand-up comedy is that you look at your life and find what's funny about it, magnify it, critique it, and even imagine how it could be different. That becomes the basis of your bit

After I consulted with the teacher and shared about my life, he suggested I try a sarcastic, self-deprecating soccer mom approach. He advised me to walk up on that stage and talk about how surreal my life can be. He told me to discuss all the weird things that happen. Needless to say, I had a lot to work with. After weeks of preparation, I'd practiced and refined my comedic stories. My brother and a few friends were in the audience, so I had some support in the crowd.

I walked on the stage and proceeded to talk about giving birth to twins (the pain, the agony, the stretch marks), share tips on surviving your kid's science project, and describe competitive soccer mom characteristics. Basically, something happens to me when I watch my children play competitive sports. I find myself yelling things like, "Don't you come outta this game unless you're bleeding or lost a tooth." One team mom gave me a lollipop to occupy my mouth if I became too loud.

To my delight, my comedy teacher was correct: people will respond positively to funny stories about your life! Also of note, the glass of red wine I gulped down prior to going on stage was a good idea. The applause was awesome, and I was so proud of myself for trying something challenging, new, and scary. It also gave me confidence to infuse humor a bit more in my presentations and interactions at work.

Sadly, other bucket list items have not been as successful. Bungee jumping resulted in me peeing my pants and learning how to use a pottery wheel meant that I created consistently misshapen bowls and pots. The point, however, is not to pursue perfection. Instead, the point is to intentionally challenge or shake up your routine. It can result in new friends, increased confidence, or maybe even some deep learning and self-reflection.

The concept of having a bucket list doesn't mean that your day-to-day life isn't meaningful or exciting. Nor should the length of your list or the items you choose be subject to critique or too much evaluation. Think about what may bring happiness or satisfaction to you or others. I think there may be some unintentional sleepwalking taking place in our lives. New experiences can awaken that part of you that has fallen asleep.

> *"The future depends on what you do today."* ~
> **Mahatma Gandhi**

CHAPTER 19

Remarriage

"Being vulnerable is the only way to allow your heart to feel true pleasure that is so real it scares you." ~ **Bob Marley**

Chapter Soundtrack: "I Belong to You" ~ Lenny Kravitz, 1998

I was not a catch. I had three kids entering challenging years—or, as I came to know them, "the hellish teenage years." I had a chronic medical condition that was in a remissive state but could rear its ugly head at times. And certainly, at forty-five, I had my own emotional baggage. I jokingly tell people that if I can find a lovely man and get married for the second time, anyone can.

I'm madly in love with this man like I never thought I could be. He's my favorite person, he gets me, and I get him. It probably shouldn't work on paper, but boy, does it! I don't quite feel myself when he's not around. It's as if there was a tangible piece of me that I didn't know was missing and found in him.

My husband is my complete opposite. He's introverted, blunt, a self-proclaimed cheap person, a world traveler, very self-disciplined, and rarely emotionally driven. He's kind, thoughtful, purposeful, dependable, and an Ivy League MBA graduate. But he'll get dirty and fix a toilet when that's required—and that's sexy! He drives an old car, loves documentaries, walked down the aisle on our wedding day to *Superfly* by Curtis Mayfield, and couldn't care less what anyone thinks of him.

He can be unexpectedly romantic. He even gets up early and cleans off my car when it snows. When my mother became ill, he turned to me and said, "Let's move her to our house so we can take care of her." He's quirky and funny and can make me laugh until I pee my pants. This is important, and it makes him a keeper. Being able to laugh with each other or at the stupid conflicts that arise will sustain a marriage.

He reminds me of my grandfather. He's a girl dad, although he and my son bond by being in the minority with four girls around them. (My husband has two daughters.) He's very patient—actually, beyond patient. It has been a true partnership in raising five unique personalities. He rolled with the punches and stayed true to himself, even if my hair was on fire daily.

He's proud and supportive of my professional accomplishments, and he encourages me to take risks. I'm a lot: a lot of energy, a lot of ideation, and a lot of talking. We've found compromise in dealing with our disparate personalities. As an introvert, he needs to decompress when he gets home from work. He simply needs to be alone. I, of course, can't wait to deconstruct my day, ask his opinion, vent about problems, and recount a joke I heard. We've decided that he needs an hour to himself. Then he'll find me (I'm sure with delight), and we can discuss our day.

It's so important to have a safe harbor and a relationship that enhances who you are. Look, I have finally grasped that unconditional love perhaps doesn't exist in romantic relationships. A true partnership and true love require compromise. To ensure the relationship stays healthy, you have to exercise patience and acceptance well beyond what you believe you're capable of doing. And this is hard because you also must be authentic and true to yourself, and not change to a false version of yourself.

> *"At 50, I began to know who I was. It was like waking up to myself."* ~ **Maya Angelou**

Another difference is that I'm financially independent in a way I wasn't during my first marriage. My husband has amazing financial acumen and is successful in his own right, but day-to-day financial dependency is not part of our partnership. Relationships are complex, but discussions or disputes around money can derail them. A couple of things to consider:

- Prenuptial agreement
    - A second marriage may necessitate protecting assets for college-age or adult children, or aging parents. Do you have a business or business assets that will need to be distributed or sold?

- Goal alignment
    - Do you have similar retirement goals? Do you give loans to family and friends?
- Budgeting
    - How much do you spend on food, clothing, and travel? How much will you save each month? How will you divide household expenses?
- Combining finances
    - Will you have a single bank account, a joint account, or separate accounts? Will you combine investments?
- Financial planning
    - Will you use a financial planner?

If you struggle to have these types of necessary discussions, you're not ready for a true partnership. That fact should be evaluated because the ability to navigate pragmatic day-to-day topics like finances or retirement plans will be necessary. Love doesn't triumph over reality.

I believe and hope that you would enter a second marriage with eyes wide open, maturity, and wisdom from experience. Do the work to ensure you have a healthy and happy relationship. Don't forget to appreciate how precious love truly is.

For more details, check out this article about money issues that could ruin your relationship.[xix]

CHAPTER 20

Critical Relationships

"My primary relationship is with myself; all others are mirrors of it. As I learn to love myself, I automatically receive the love and appreciation that I desire from others. If I am committed to myself and to living my truth, I will attract others with equal commitment. My willingness to be intimate with my own deep feelings creates the space for intimacy with another. As I learn to love myself, I receive the love I desire from others." ~ **Shakti Gawain**

Chapter Soundtrack: "Feeling Good" ~ Nina Simone, 1964

As an extrovert, I have lots of acquaintances. But realistically, I have only a few close friends. One very important thing to note is who among your friends actually shows up when you need them. There are friends who, when you share that you are ill, say, "I hope you feel better." But then there is the friend who rings your doorbell with soup and decongestants. There's also that friend who, when you say you're struggling with your teenager, extends an invitation for that grumpy hormonal teen to come and stay the weekend with them.

My best friend, Stacy, has seen me through all of my ups and downs and has always been unselfish and caring. And she's been a steadfast auntie to my children. One example of the type of support I've received from Stacy was when I separated from my first husband. She moved in with me and helped all of us during that stressful transition.

> *"Lots of people want to ride with you in the limo—what you want is someone who will take the bus with you when the limo breaks down."*
> ~ **Oprah Winfrey**

I often use my relationship with Stacy to illustrate for my children what is healthy in friendships. I tell them they don't need to travel with a crowd of so-called friends. Be discerning and notice the person who's thoughtful and loyal, gets your jokes, and sees your enemies as their enemies. This extends to professional relationships as well. Your trust has immense value, so don't give it away easily.

A true friend in business gives you candid and honest professional feedback. This friend shares their network with you and thinks about you when opportunities arise. They remind you of your strengths and gifts, and they encourage your aspirations. This type of friendship can be tested during business challenges or even when competing interests occur. However, if this friend demonstrates how much they value your relationship despite opportunities to devalue it, that's trust.

Not all critical relationships are those with lifelong friends. They can also encompass your family, spirituality, and, of course, yourself. I have written much about family, but those connections are going to be present, good or bad, and managing and even cherishing them is key. Family is like a touchstone, a link to your past and shared experiences. I caution you to not take family for granted, as parts of your identity reside with each family member.

My Aunt Nina is another key relationship for me. She's my mother's youngest sister, and only eleven years separate us. As a young child I followed her around, amazed by her teenage coolness. I felt loved by her always. As we both have gotten older, she has become a friend—and now at times, a stand-in mother figure. Patient and thoughtful, she sends silly cards and gifts to me and the kids for no reason. We speak several times a week about politics, home décor, and the strange things our kids do. She hates to fly but will get on a plane when anyone needs her. I wish everyone could have her as an auntie.

Another important thing is how you ground yourself in something larger. Spirituality is a complex notion—and I don't specifically mean whether you believe in God or some type of deity. I think of spirituality as a belief in a greater purpose and a need at times to believe in the unknown. It can even be an inherent belief in good being triumphant over evil. During times when we bear witness to tragedy, violence, and loss, that belief is likely what keeps many of us sane.

But your most important and critical relationship is with yourself. And having a healthy relationship with yourself takes work and investment. This may be the hardest relationship to make and keep healthy. Self-love should be easy, but it's not. Whether it's personal appearance, professional success, or even a romantic relationship, it's hard to measure up to your own expectations.

Meditation has helped me with this. I create positive affirmations and learn how to manage those negative, intrusive thoughts that many of us struggle with. I find quiet time in the morning and evening to essentially quiet my mind and do a mental cleanse.

> *"Keep your best wishes, close to your heart and watch what happens."* ~ **Tony DeLiso, *Legacy: The Power Within***

CHAPTER 21

Being Gentle with Yourself

"Talk to yourself like you would to someone you love." ~ **Brené Brown**

Chapter Soundtrack: "Golden" ~ Jill Scott, 2004

This may be the most important thing that I have learned in life: Be gentle with yourself. Forgive yourself. Look in the mirror and tell yourself you're worthy. I have come across so many people who have an active inner critic. This is that voice that tells you that you're not good enough, people don't think highly of you, you should be more successful, etc.

This is true for CEOs, nuns, children, your colleagues, your neighbors. Yes, I coached a former nun, and her dedication to her faith and community still was accompanied by an identity crisis. The only exception might be Beyonce. She may not have low self-esteem in any form. The point here is that regardless of the position you hold in your company, the house you own, and the money in your bank account, you may have some type of inner struggle going on.

Your struggle can exist in all forms, including health (physical and mental), helplessly watching your child struggling academically, even career instability. We simply have no control over what each day may bring. Adopting a positive, pragmatic, and adaptable mindset is key—particularly when you understand that this is also a reality of everyone around you.

We need to accept our imperfections and life's curveballs. Oh, the mistakes I have made, witnessed, or counseled others through. Here are a few suggestions:

- Take some time each day to breathe and practice gratitude. It can be a walk you take mid-day or in the evening while listening to music.
    - When feeling really depleted, I like to make a list of the people and things I'm grateful for.
        - I'm grateful for my loving husband, beautiful children, family and friends.
        - I'm grateful that I have the ability to support my family financially.
        - I'm grateful to have survived a worldwide pandemic.
        - I'm grateful for Starbucks coffee.

- Evaluate and prioritize what is truly important to you.
    - Ask a trusted friend or mentor for advice or feedback if you need assistance with this exercise.
    - Work with a coach. This focused time to align desire with actions or simply to explore your why can change your life.
- Your mental health must be cared for. If you engage in patterns that are harmful or self-destructive, DO NOT PASS GO. Schedule time with a therapist and prioritize this time to work on you.
- Are you surrounded by people who enhance your life? If not, consider whom you spend time with and how they're not enhancing your life. Positive energy creates more positive energy, and negative energy creates more negative energy. It really is that simple.
    - I'm not suggesting this is easy but do some self-reflection on whom you welcome and keep around. Basically, remove the assholes in your life.
- Love yourself the most. That's not selfish. Your well-being should be your first priority. It allows you to be a better partner, parent, leader, and friend.

"Only kind people are truly tolerant.

Only gentle people are truly strong."

~ **Cathy Burnham Martin**, *Encouragement: How to Be and Find the Best*

PART 5

In Conclusion

CHAPTER 22

Putting It All Together

"I really don't think life is about the I-could-have-beens. Life is only about the I-tried-to-do. I don't mind the failure but I can't imagine that I'd forgive myself if I didn't try." ~ **Nikki Giovanni**

Chapter Soundtrack: "Just Fine" ~ Mary J. Blige, 2007

I know that my journey still has twists and turns waiting for me in the future. However, I hope that my story of what has happened thus far can be a guide, an ah-ha moment, or even a point of reflection. But here's the thing: if I can have a life full of joy, fulfillment, and love, you can too.

A few life truth bombs I try to live by:

- Your childhood doesn't define you. It can inspire you, inform your choices, and provide perspective. But you get to decide your path.
- When you say you're sorry, mean it. Then don't repeat the thing that prompted the apology.

- Purposefully seek connection in your life. It can be connection to people, the arts, nature, etc. Find the things that replenish you. This is how you build reserves to deal with the inevitable bullshit that will come your way.
- Spend time with your elders. If you don't have parents or grandparents living, borrow a close friend's relatives. They may have some wisdom to provide to you.
- Spend time with people younger than you and really listen to their perspectives. They likely see the world differently, and we need to listen to help create a viable future for them.
- Reach back, give back, or volunteer if you're in a position to do so. It changes how you think about yourself. The juxtaposition of helping those less fortunate than you—mentoring children, for example—triggers your appreciation for what you have in your life.
- Take the occasional long bath. Bubbles are not optional. Think of nothing but your strengths and those you love and care about.
- Keep learning. Anyone who knows me expects to receive TED Talks, links to articles that I think may be insightful, or a song from an artist I just discovered. Read books. Don't get all your information from one news source. Travel and learn about other cultures. Challenge yourself.

- Follow some thought-provoking folks on Twitter. I learn something new every day and often can glean some interesting concepts or ideas.

I used to give people advice on how to fit in and to move up the corporate ladder by being a political animal and simply working harder than peers. To some degree there's still validity in that counsel. However, my perspective has shifted. Maybe that comes with time and experience.

For example, if women keep following the path laid out in front of them, some studies show it will be many, many years before there is gender parity in the C-suite or on boards. I now say be fearless, advocate for yourself, challenge the status quo, and push hard for what you want. It reminds me of the title of Laurel Thatcher Ulrich's 2007 book: *Well-behaved Women Seldom Make History*.

Imagine what doesn't exist and create the job you want. Be entrepreneurial, have a side hustle so you're never forced to compromise in a way that hurts your soul. I often juggle multiple projects or endeavors at the same time. I like having the choice in how I build my brand and finances. Think on this. You may be surprised at what you can accomplish when you leverage your strengths.

Your professional career is interwoven with your personal life. There's no getting away from it. I love what I do and feel blessed to have a career that has challenged and rewarded me. It's important to pursue a career that suits you and plays to your strengths—one that allows you to be authentic.

As hard as it may be at times, circle back to joy and all the things that replenish you. That's what realizing your potential truly is: the ability to accept what has happened in life that cannot be changed, learn from it, and love who you are because of or despite it.

I truly hope you live the life you deserve.

> *"Find the place inside yourself where nothing is impossible."* ~ **Deepak Chopra**

Before You Go

Thank you for sharing this journey with me as you read this book. I hope it stimulated hope in you and helped you to realize you can learn greatly from your past and, as a result stay, motivated to reach your goals. I wish you nothing but happiness and fulfillment in your life. I'd like to take just a few more minutes to make a request. It's not a large one.

If you enjoyed this book, could you please take a moment, go to Amazon (www.amazon.com), and look up this title, ***Potential, Leverage Your Past For The Professional and Personal Success You Deserve*** and leave a short review? Even if you only had time to go through a couple of chapters, you will be able to leave a review and, if you desire, go back later, and add to it once you've had a chance to complete the book. Even your first impressions are very useful.

Books succeed by thoughtful readers who take time to leave honest reviews. Share what the book meant to you and what strategies you can use. This is how other readers learn about books that are most beneficial for them to buy. I thank you in advance for this very kind gesture of appreciation. It means the world to me.

Finally please reach out to me at www.amplifypeopleadvisors.com if you would like to receive valuable information on reaching your full potential.

With gratitude,

Barbara

Acknowledgements

There are too many people to thank but I will try to sum it up!

The foundation of this book is my upbringing - every inspiring, loving, challenging and messy event. To Leo and Anna Mae Smith, my maternal grandparents who deeply influenced me as a child and as an adult – thank you for the life lessons I use every day.

To my brother who has been my lifelong companion and confidant who said," I am sure whatever you write will be great!"

To my children and the many lessons, they continue to teach me about patience, the unexpected, and this new world we are trying to survive and thrive in – I hope this book gives you some insight to your mom.

To my friends who help me navigate all life's challenges and celebrate all the good stuff with me – much love...

To my business colleagues - there are too many to individually mention. I thank you for your support, mentorship, and friendship.

Thank you to Melissa G Wilson, my publisher and book coach, who helped guide me through this writing experience of blending the story of my personal and professional life and my desire to help others.

Thank you to my husband who loves me for both for my strengths and my weaknesses and always tells me to speak my truth.

Some may say my father never realized his potential due to his chaotic, funny, and tragic life but this book is a testimony of the potential he unwittingly instilled in me.

Lastly, my mother whom I miss everyday nurtured my curious, intense, quirky personality and simply wanted me to reach my potential...peace.

About the Author

Barbara is a senior executive with more than twenty-five years of operations and human resources leadership, DEI, and board governance experience. Barbara is the Chief Administrative Officer at the John F. Kennedy Center for the Performing Arts. She previously held leadership positions at the National Restaurant Association, American Red Cross, Ellucian, and XO Communications. She has a BA in political science from Rutgers University and completed graduate coursework at Harvard Business School, American University, and the University of Maryland. Barbara is also an ICF-certified executive coach.

A proven leader who has consistently delivered exceptional results by deploying creative and cost-effective business initiatives, Barbara is also known for building high-performing teams and finding exceptional talent. Barbara has broad expertise in diversity, equity, and inclusion (DEI), as well as leadership development.

She has varied board leadership experience. She is currently a member of the Board of Directors for Hershey Entertainment & Resorts. HE&R is a privately held entertainment and hospitality company.

Additionally, Barbara is currently a board member of the Lupus Foundation of America and serves as secretary. Previously, she was a director on the Women's Food-service Forum Board. WFF is the foodservice industry's premier leadership development organization with more than twenty-five years of experience advancing women in the food industry.

Self-Study Guide

Chapter 1—Starting at the Beginning

- Is marrying young a curse or a blessing, and why?
    - What are the pros and cons of marrying your high-school sweetheart versus waiting until your thirties or later?
    - Have you ever been in a relationship that you look back on with regrets? Or fondness?
        - If you answered yes to this question, what were three memories you have regarding the relationship or relationships?
- What role do you think family played in Lorraine's life? What role does family play in your life?
- What are your expectations around family in terms of support, child-rearing, financial support, advice?
- Does it take a village (family) to raise a child?

Chapter 2—Mom

- What factors do women (or men) have to consider when leaving an abusive relationship?
- How did the racism Barbara experienced as a child shape her?

- Relationships between mothers and their children are intimate and complex. Do you see parallels or differences between Barbara's story and your relationship with your mother?

Chapter 3—Dad – Yes, I Have Daddy Issues

- How do you feel about Robert violently responding to his son being struck by his stepfather? What feelings from his own childhood may have motivated him? Have you experienced similar violence in your family? If yes, how has it impacted your choices?
    - Is love an excuse to be violent or respond violently to another?
- Unrealized potential is woven into this chapter. What path did you hope Robert would take after his prison term?
    - Can people find redemption or positive change after prison?
    - Can people change? Do they change easily?
    - What keeps most people from changing their lives dramatically? Think:
        - Prison
        - Addiction
        - Divorce
        - Poverty
- Although estranged from her father, Barbara consistently came to the rescue. What would you have done?
    - Is rescuing someone healthy or dysfunctional?

  - If rescuing someone means risking our own job, career, family, or life, should we do it? Is it okay to be selfish and focus on our own family first?
  - What is the difference between carrying someone and helping someone?
  - Is tough love a good thing? Should people suffer the consequences of their choices and decisions?

Chapter 4—Grandparents

  - What role have grandparents played in your life?
  - Why were Barbara's grandparents so significant in hers?
  - How does religion or ritual, like going to church, connect family members?

Chapter 5—Brother

- Why is the bond so close between Barbara and Robbie?
- Why was she so protective of him?
- How do you think Robbie's childhood recollections are different from Barbara's?

Chapter 6—Life Away from Home

- Why do you think Barbara was eager to go away to school?

    - Does changing homes, neighborhoods, or jobs solve our problems, or do our problems stay with us no matter where we go?
- Can you imagine attending boarding school?
    - What do you think your biggest challenge would be?
    - How easily do you think you could make friends? Why?
- How do you think this impacted Barbara and Robbie?

Chapter 7—Stories of College Life

- What was your college experience like? How did it change you?
    - Did you associate with mostly Black friends, mostly White friends, or a pretty even mix? Why or why not?
- Were you intimidated by all the changes, like making new friends and handling academic pressures?
    - Did you have family, friends, a therapist, counselor, professor, or mentors to help you with the changes?
        - How did those people make the biggest impact in your life?
- Looking back, what would you do differently?
    - If you worked during college, would you not work?
    - If you didn't work during college, would you get a job?
    - Would you take a gap year and work or travel rather than go directly into college?

Chapter 8—The First Job

- What was your first job like?
- What did you learn?
- Were you able to build close relationships with coworkers?
- What would you tell this younger version of yourself to do? Or not do?

Chapter 9—Marriage and Divorce

- Do you have daddy or mommy issues? How have they impacted your relationship choices?
- Do women have different expectations than men about marriage?
- Did children change the dynamic in your marriage?
- Should parents stay together for the sake of the children, or should they divorce and work on making sure the children are still raised by both parents in a loving and supportive arrangement?
- Should both parents always have custody?

Chapter 10—Single Motherhood: A Whole Different Ball Game

- Describe the number-one challenge of being a single mother.
- Name three ways you could help a single mother you know.
- How would you feel about speaking up at work about challenges you face as a single mother, like work schedules, sick days, etc.?

- Do single fathers have as hard a time working and managing a household as mothers? Why or in what ways?

Chapter 11—How to Negotiate: Knowing Your Worth

- Why is it difficult to discuss money or negotiate salaries?
    - Looking back, if you found it was difficult to discuss, what could you have done differently?
    - Do you agree that women struggle with these conversations more than men?
- What needs to happen so women are paid as competitively as men?

Chapter 12—The Professional Arc

- What is your personal brand?
    - Does it reflect who you are authentically?
    - How do you think people see you?
        - At work?
        - At home?
    - Have you experienced imposter syndrome?
    - Have you experienced microaggressions at work?
        - What did you do?
    - How do you typically handle professional or personal obstacles or conflicts?
    - Are you investing in yourself? If so, in what way? If not, what options could you explore?

Chapter 13—Role Model: Burden or Gift?

- Have you experienced being viewed as a role model?
    - How do you view it? Burden or gift?
    - Who has been a role model for you?
        - Why?
    - Have you ever been let down by someone you viewed as a role model?

Chapter 14—How to Talk About Diversity, Equity, and Inclusion (DEI)

- List the top three most difficult topics people hate to discuss.
    - Rank these topics in order of hardest to discuss:
        - Money
        - Sex
        - Race
        - Religion
        - Politics
        - Career choices
        - Salary
        - Child-rearing policies
        - Relationships
        - Bad habits (smoking, spending habits, etc.)
        - Saving and spending habits

Chapter 15—Facing Your Fears

- What is the number-one fear you have about your personal life?

- What is the number-one fear you have about your professional/work life?
- How do you face your fears? Do you read self-help books, see a therapist, or talk to friends or a spouse? What helps you face and overcome your fears?

Chapter 16—Wheel of Fortune

- If you knew you couldn't fail at it, what would you do for a career?
- Are you always learning, sometimes learning, or done with learning? Why?
- Can you name one or two opportunities you'd like to take but are afraid to take, think you can't afford, or don't have the time for?
- Are you a risk taker? Why or why not?
- Describe the last time you did something out of character, something you normally wouldn't do, or a risk you wouldn't take.

Chapter 17 — When Your Body Lets You Down

- How has your body let you down?
- Have you forgiven your body for letting you down? It has served you for many years, and now it's not able to. Can you be accepting of that? Why or why not?
- When ill health, an accident, or other event happens that restricts your ability to work, raise a

family, or enjoy life like before, how can you turn that change into something positive? How do you find the silver lining?

  - Do you find a silver lining? Why or why not?

Chapter 18—Bucket List

- Do you have a bucket list? Why or why not?
- Is a bucket list a good thing to have? Why or why not?
- If you have one or were to make one, name five things that are or would be on your bucket list.
- If you're married, name five things that are on your partner's bucket list.
- If you're single or have kids, name five things on a friend's or your children's bucket list.
- Do you continually revise and/or add things to your list?

Chapter 19—Remarriage

- Do you think second marriages are better than first marriages?
- Is the term *starter marriage* a true description of a first marriage? Do we learn things in a first marriage that help in a subsequent marriage?
- What makes any marriage—first, second, third, or whatever—work?
- What are the three things that you think make a marriage fail?

Chapter 20—Critical Relationships

- Who are the people you consider to be your closest friends?
- What qualities are deal breakers when considering someone a best friend?
- What are the qualities you seek in a critical relationship?
- Are the qualities needed in a good a work relationship the same as those needed in a personal relationship?
    - Can a work friend also be a personal friend?

Chapter 21—Being Gentle with Yourself

- Many of us want others to be gentle with us when and where we're unable to be gentle with ourselves. How do you want others to be gentle with you?
- How are you gentle with yourself?
- Where do you carve out time to take care of yourself, even when and if it means not taking care of others? For instance, taking a much-needed nap rather than going shopping with a friend or playing with a child.
- List five or more ways you're gentle with yourself now. Then list five more ways you can be gentle with yourself in the future.

Chapter 22—Putting it All Together

- How has Barbara incorporated lessons from her childhood or college years into who she is today? Give three examples of how you've turned lemons into lemonade in your own life.
- What major lessons or insights have you learned in reading this book or looking back at your own life lessons that you'd pass on to a younger person?
- What do you think has been your greatest accomplishment so far? Marriage? Children? Career? List the three things you consider to be major accomplishments and why you're proud of them.

Endnotes

I - Parker, Kim and Stepler, Renee. "As U.S. marriage rate hovers at 505, education gap in marital status widens." Pew Research Center. September 14, 2017. https://www.pewresearch.org/fact-tank/2017/09/14/as-u-s-marriage-rate-hovers-at-50-education-gap-in-marital-status-widens/#:~:text=In%202016%2C%20the%20median%20age,rising%20steadily%20in%20recent%20decades.

II - Rakovec-Felser, Zlatka. "Domestic Violence and Abuse in Intimate Relationship from Public Health Perspective." NCBI. Accessed August 4, 2021. https://www.ncbi.nlm.nih.gov/pmc/articles/PMC4768593/

III - Anderson, Jane. "The impact of family structure on the health of children: Effects of divorce." NCBI. Accessed August 4, 2021. https://www.ncbi.nlm.nih.gov/pmc/articles/PMC4240051/

IV - Local Government Commission website. "The Role of Local Government in Creating Healthy, Livable Neighborhoods." Lgc.org. Accessed August 4, 2021. https://www.lgc.org/resource/community-gardens/

V - Angrish, Dhruvika. "How community gardens are tackling food insecurity." Blnkpage.org. Accessed August 4, 2021. http://home.blnkpage.org/health-science/how-community-gardens-are-tackling-food-insecurity/

VI -Marquardt, Elizabeth. "Between Two Worlds: The Inner Lives Of Children Of Divorce." Amazon.com. Accessed August 4, 2021. https://www.amazon.com/Between-Two-Worlds-Children-Divorce/dp/0307237117

VII - Clark, K. B., & Clark, M. K. (1939). The development of consciousness of self and the emergence of racial identification in Negro preschool children. *The Journal of Social Psychology*, 10, 591–599. Accessed August 4, 2021. https://doi.org/10.1080/00224545.1939.9713394

VIII - Lander, Laura, Howsare, Janie and Byrne, Marilyn. "The Impact of Substance Use Disorders on Families and Children: From Theory to Practice." NCBI. Accessed August 4, 2021. https://www.ncbi.nlm.nih.gov/pmc/articles/PMC3725219/

IX -Wikipedia. "Destabilisation." Wikipedia.org. Accessed August 4, 2021. https://en.wikipedia.org/wiki/Destabilisation

X - ASA website. "Women More Likely Than Men to Initiate Divorces, But Not Non-Marital Breakups." American Sociological Association. Accessed August 4, 2021. https://www.asanet.org/press-center/press-releases/women-more-likely-men-initiate-divorces-not-non-marital-breakups

XI - Statista.com website. "Number of children living with a single mother or a single father in the U.S. from 1970 to 2019." Statista.com. Accessed August 4, 2021. https://www.statista.com/statistics/252847/

number-of-children-living-with-a-single-mother-or-single-father/

XII - TED: The Economics Daily. "Baby boomers born from 1957 to 1964 held an average of 12.3 jobs from ages 18 to 52." Bls.gov. August 27, 2019. https://www.bls.gov/opub/ted/2019/baby-boomers-born-from-1957-to-1964-held-an-average-of-12-point-3-jobs-from-ages-18-to-52.htm#:~:text=Bureau%20of%20Labor%20Statistics,-The%20Economics%20Daily&text=People%20born%20from%201957%20to,from%20ages%2018%20to%2052.

XIII - Oxford Learner's Dictionaries. "karma" definition. Oxfordlearnersdictionaries.com. Accessed August 4, 2021. https://www.oxfordlearnersdictionaries.com/us/definition/american_english/karma#:~:text=karma-,noun,them%20in%20the%20next%20life

XIV - Vanderbilt University website. "Unconscious Bias." Vanderbilt.edu. Accessed August 4, 2021. https://www.vanderbilt.edu/diversity/unconscious-bias/

XV - Mohr, Tara Sophia. "Why Women Don't Apply for Jobs Unless They're 100% Qualified." HBR. Accessed August 4, 2021. https://hbr.org/2014/08/why-women-dont-apply-for-jobs-unless-theyre-100-qualified

XVI - Batish, Amit. Q4 2020 Equilar Gender Diversity Index: Gender Parity on Russell 3000 Boards Projected by 2032." Equilar.com. March 3, 2021. https://www.

equilar.com/reports/78-q4-2020-equilar-gender-diversity-index.html

XVII - CDC.gov. "Systemic Lupus Erythematosus (SLE)." Cdc.gov. Accessed August 4, 2021.

https://www.cdc.gov/lupus/facts/detailed.html#:~:text=Systemic%20lupus%20erythematosus%20(SLE)%2C,%2C%20kidneys%2C%20and%20blood%20vessels.

XVIII - Ibid.

XIX - Bieber, Christy. "5 Money Issues That Could Ruin Your Relationship." The Ascent. September 10, 2019. https://www.fool.com/the-ascent/banks/articles/5-money-issues-that-could-ruin-your-relationship/

Made in the USA
Coppell, TX
22 December 2021

69885890R00105